THE WOLF

Look for these and other books in the
Lucent Endangered Animals and Habitats series:

The Elephant
The Giant Panda
The Oceans
The Rhinoceros
The Shark
The Whale
The Wolf

Other related titles in the Lucent Overview series:

Acid Rain
Endangered Species
Energy Alternatives
Garbage
The Greenhouse Effect
Hazardous Waste
Ocean Pollution
Oil Spills
Ozone
Pesticides
Population
Rainforests
Recycling
Vanishing Wetlands
Zoos

THE WOLF

BY HAYLEY R. MITCHELL

Endangered
Animals &
Habitats

LUCENT BOOKS, INC.
SAN DIEGO, CALIFORNIA

LUCENT *Overview Series*

Library of Congress Cataloging-in-Publication Data

Mitchell, Hayley R., 1968–
    The wolf / by Hayley R. Mitchell.
        p.   cm. — (Endangered animals & habitats)
    Includes bibliographical references (p.   ) and index.
    Summary: Discusses the habits, habitat, and endangered status
of the wolf, as well as its place in human society.
    ISBN 1-56006-252-5 (lib. : alk. paper)
    1. Canis—Juvenile literature.   2. Wolves—Juvenile literature.
3. Endangered species—Juvenile literature. [1. Wolves.
2. Endangered species.] I. Title. II. Series.
QL737.C22M58   1998
599'.773—dc21
                                        97-51586
                                            CIP
                                            AC

Contents

Introduction

THE ISSUE OF wolf endangerment is multifaceted, complicated, in part, because wolves are classified into a number of different species. Some of these species, such as the gray wolf, can be healthy and thriving in one region but still be listed as threatened or endangered in a different region where their population numbers have dwindled. Some wolf species' numbers are so low that they remain on the brink of extinction; other wolf species have disappeared completely.

Where the wolves roamed

Historically, healthy populations of wolves roamed anywhere that they could find food to support themselves. In the United States during the 1600s, for example, wolf populations lived in the grasslands, the Arctic highlands, the deserts of Arizona and New Mexico, the forests of the Northwest, and the plains of Texas and Louisiana.

Human settlement and development greatly reduced the number of free-roaming wolves. In the United States, once-abundant wolf populations began to shrink in size as settlers carried out mass extermination campaigns that sought to protect livestock from wolf attacks. By the 1970s, nearly all the wolves had disappeared in the lower forty-eight states, an area that once made up 95 percent of the wolf's territory. And the United States is not the only nation that has lost its wolves. Wolf populations have dwindled worldwide.

The wolf is extinct in most of Europe, including England, Ireland, Scotland, and the Netherlands. The majority of the wolf populations that remain in Europe exist in very small numbers. As of 1995, for instance, only 5 wolves lived in Germany and France, approximately 150 inhabited Portugal, and 500 resided in Bulgaria, Greece, and the former Yugoslavia.

Just a few of the wolf species that are extinct in the world today as a result of extermination programs or habitat destruction include *alces,* the Kenai Peninsula wolf of Alaska, extinct since 1925; *bernardi,* a white wolf of the Victoria Islands in the Arctic, extinct since 1952; *fuscus,* the brown wolf of the Cascade Mountains, extinct since

Wolves, like the gray wolf pictured here, once roamed freely in abundant numbers, but some wolf species are now extinct and other wolf populations have dwindled worldwide.

1940; *mogollonensis,* a medium-sized wolf of Arizona and New Mexico, extinct since 1935; *nubilus,* the "buffalo wolf" of the Great Plains, extinct since 1926; and *youngi,* a light brown wolf of the southern Rocky Mountains, extinct since 1935.

Endangered and threatened wolves

Wolf species that are not extinct but whose numbers are so small that future extinction is likely without some kind of human intervention are listed as endangered or threatened under the Endangered Species Act. Wolves currently listed under the act include the gray wolf, Mexican wolf, red wolf, and Ethiopian wolf. These populations of wolves decreased for a variety of reasons. Extermination campaigns have played the largest role in each species' diminishment, but sport hunting, trapping, habitat destruction, and interbreeding with other canids have also contributed to losses.

Canis lupus, the gray wolf, once ranged from coast to coast and from Canada to Mexico in the continental United States. Today the gray wolf covers very little of this original range. While populations of wolves still survive, their numbers vary depending on availability of food and on competition between wolf packs. In 1995, approximately 15 wolves resided in Idaho, 70 in Michigan, 60–90 in Montana, 5 in Washington, and 55 in Wisconsin. The gray wolf is listed as threatened (likely to become endangered in the near future) in Minnesota, where an estimated 2,000 wolves survive.

A subspecies of the gray wolf, *Canis lupus baileyi,* also known as El Lobo, or the Mexican wolf, is one of the rarest wolves in existence. These wolves once lived freely in oak woodlands of Arizona, New Mexico, Texas, and Mexico. Currently, a small number of Mexican wolves survive in captive breeding programs, but they are no longer known to live in the wild.

Classified as a separate species from the gray wolf, the red wolf, *Canis rufus,* is capable of adapting to a variety of habitats that provide heavy vegetation. Before its endangerment, the red wolf could be found as far north as Pennsylvania and as far west as central Texas. By the late 1930s, red wolf populations had dwindled, inhabiting only areas of southern Louisiana and southeastern Texas, and mountain regions of Arkansas, Oklahoma, and Missouri. By the early 1980s, the red wolf was considered extinct in the wild, but small populations have made a slow comeback through reintroduction programs.

Another species of critically endangered wolves is *Canis simensis,* the rare Ethiopian, or Abyssinian, wolf. The Ethiopian wolf is the only true wolf species in Africa. It lives in mountain enclaves of the Ethiopian Highlands. Studies in 1995 estimated that only five hundred Ethiopian wolves remain in existence; the largest population inhabits the Bale Mountains National Park in southern Ethiopia, and nearby glacial valleys. Captive breeding has been described as essential for the survival of the species and for the preservation of its genetic purity, but breeding efforts have not yet begun.

The Ethiopian wolf is listed as endangered by the International Union for the Conservation of Nature and Natural Resources (IUCN). The IUCN also recognizes the red wolf as being endangered in the wild; the gray wolf receives international protection as well.

Healthy wolf populations

The largest wolf populations today live in forested regions, often in hilly, rugged terrain of the Northern Hemisphere far from populated communities. The healthiest U.S. populations of wolves live in Alaska, with five thousand to eight thousand wolves occupying 95 percent of their historical range. More than fifty thousand wolves survive in Canada despite having been eliminated from 15 percent of their range. Outside of Alaska and Canada, the largest population of wolves can be found in the former Soviet Union, where approximately ninety thousand wolves survive.

Although wolf populations in these regions are thriving, with plenty to eat and vast space in which to roam, environmentalists worry about their future. Wolves are still

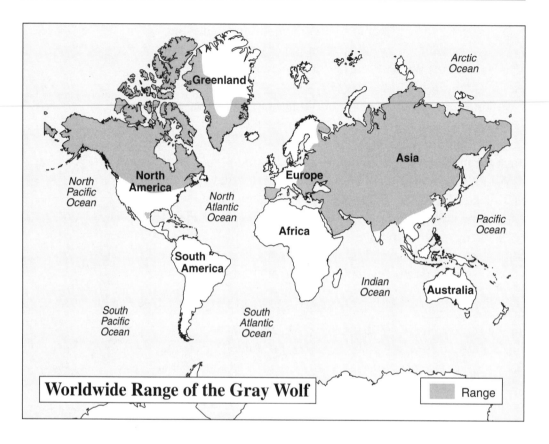

Worldwide Range of the Gray Wolf

Range

widely hunted in the former Soviet Union, for example, and they also remain the targets of mass extermination campaigns in both Canada and Alaska. Since these kinds of campaigns once contributed to the endangerment or extinction of abundant wolves elsewhere, there are concerns that history may repeat itself.

Saving the wolf

In addition to protections offered by the Endangered Species Act, efforts are under way to restore and provide wolf habitat in national parks and on other lands. Captive breeding programs and reintroduction efforts are also working to raise wolf population levels in the wild.

Wolf protection and restoration efforts, however, have not received universal support. These efforts are sometimes seen as belittling human needs and as a means of restricting land rights, and sometimes costing people their jobs. Other points of opposition include the cost of expensive wolf reintroduction programs and the threat wolves may pose to human safety.

Environmentalists believe that wolves and other endangered species are worth saving and that wolf habitats, often destroyed and exploited for human needs, should also be protected by law. Those in favor of governmental preservation efforts also point to the importance of maintaining biodiversity.

Biodiversity refers collectively to the various plants and animals and their habitats that make up the earth. Biodiversity is threatened every time a species dies out, because some species function as food for other species. Therefore, if a species becomes extinct, a second species may starve and also become extinct if it is unable to adapt to the food-chain change in its environment. Those concerned about maintaining biodiversity feel that all species have an intrinsic right to exist. Humankind, they believe, should make a conscious effort to maintain the habitats of the world's species, and it has a moral obligation to protect those species in danger of extinction.

1

Demystifying the Wolf

WOLVES ARE CONSIDERED predators. Like grizzly bears and mountain lions, wolves are animals that survive by killing and eating other animals. Throughout history, humans have feared the wolf for its predatory nature and have viewed it as a menace to society. It is this view of the wolf that has led to mass wolf exterminations in the past and opposition to wolf protection programs today.

Much of the fear of wolves probably stems more from legends than from any real incidents of wolves threatening human life. Numerous well-known fables, superstitions, and fairy tales dating as far back as 600 B.C. depict the wolf as being cunning and deceitful. Aesop's fables, such as "The Wolf and the Lamb," "The Wolf and the Crane," and "The Boy Who Cried Wolf," illustrate conniving wolf characters that take advantage of the weak to fulfill their own appetites. Later children's stories such as "Little Red Riding Hood" and "The Three Little Pigs" also include wolf villains. During the Middle Ages, wolves were feared not only for their predatory nature, but also for the magical powers they were thought to possess. For example, many people believed that wolf meat was poisonous and that a gaze from a wolf could cause blindness.

Are wolves just misunderstood?

Although wolves have been portrayed as vicious creatures, in reality they pose very little threat to humans.

"SAY, AREN'T YOU ON THE ENDANGERED SPECIES LIST?"

Wolves are naturally shy animals that prefer not to stray into populated areas. Although there have been reports of human injury caused by wolf attack, according to author Nancy Jo Tubbs, there are "no documented accounts in North American history of a healthy, wild wolf attacking and killing a human."[1]

Biologists and other wildlife specialists say that domesticated dogs pose a greater threat to people than wolves. As editor Rick McIntyre explains, "Since dogs kill an average of twenty people and injure another five hundred thousand annually, they are far more dangerous than wolves."[2]

Those who have studied wolves at close range say they demonstrate a remarkable acceptance of and curiosity about outsiders as long as they do not feel threatened. When *National Geographic* photographer Jim Brandenburg studied wolves for a full summer on Ellesmere Island, the northernmost point in North America, located in Canada's Northwest Territories, he did not feel threatened by the pack; in fact, he felt welcomed by it.

Because they had not learned to fear humans in their isolated region, the wolves of Ellesmere did not view Brandenburg as a threat to their existence. Thus, they allowed him to photograph their daily lives and even trusted him to remain outside their pup dens while the pack went hunting. The wolves also did not seem bothered when Brandenburg followed them on hunts in his all-terrain vehicle.

Life in the pack

Though shy toward humans, wolves are social creatures among themselves. The collaborative nature of wolves, their instinct for working together, is what helps them function within the pack. Wolf packs are generally made up of a dominant male and female wolf, known as the alpha pair, their offspring, and often adult siblings. The dominant wolves reign over the rest of the pack, which can reach up to thirty-six members in size. The average pack consists of eight or fewer wolves, but red wolf packs are generally even smaller, consisting of the adult pair and one or two offspring of the current and previous years.

Just as in human family units, wolves form strong bonds with other pack members. Male wolves, for instance, seldom leave their own packs to join others. In addition to being devoted, wolves have been described as friendly, affectionate, and helpful toward each other, and happy for the companionship of pack members. Author Robert Busch explains that "pack members will often greet each other nose to nose, with wagging tails and whole bodies wriggling with joy."[3]

Who's the boss?

Social ranking within wolf packs may change as wolves sexually mature, reach old age, or become ill or wounded.

The ranking of the alpha pair is established not by age or size, however, but by the wolves' adoption and maintenance of dominant body postures and movements. Dominant postures of the wolf in charge include walking with the head held high and a partly erect tail. Dominant wolves are known to stare down subordinate wolves; they may also nip and bite them and pin them to the ground while baring their teeth. Dominant wolves also enjoy more breeding and feeding rights than other members of the pack. For example, they are the first to eat at kills. Like true leaders, they are also the first to attack in confrontations with other wolf packs.

Subordinate wolves, on the other hand, exhibit submissive posturing in the presence of dominant wolves. These postures may include a lowering of the tail, folding back of the ears, crouching, and whining. In extreme submission, a subordinate wolf may even urinate on itself. Busch explains that, though these "ritual gestures appear vicious, they actually serve to preserve pack cohesion without bloodshed."[4]

These gray wolves in Canada are part of a typical wolf pack. Most of the wolves' daily tasks are accomplished together.

Wolves may show their possession of a fresh kill by engaging in dominant postures, such as snarling and baring their teeth.

When aggression does occur within the wolf pack, it is often focused on the omega wolf. This wolf is the lowest ranked wolf in the pack, and it is frequently physically harassed and intimidated by the other wolves. Sometimes the omega wolf feels so intimidated that it will leave the pack and become a lone wolf. Lone wolves make up only 15 percent of the wolf population. Without the support and protection of the pack, their mortality rates are high. Unless they are successful in joining another pack, they are often unable to catch enough prey to live on.

The omega wolf is not the only object of wolf pack aggression. Aggression may occur between packs when one encroaches on another's territory. Wolf packs are most likely to come in contact with each other when food is scarce and they have wandered outside their usual territories in search of it.

Home is where the scent is

A wolf's territory is its home. Even when hunting, wolves usually stay within the land they have marked as their own. Their activities on this land change throughout the year in accordance with the seasons. In the spring and summer months, wolves remain fairly stationary. They stay close to their dens or homesites to care for new pups. In the fall and winter the wolves are nomadic, traveling and hunting as a pack.

Wolf packs mark large areas of land as their hunting territory by urinating, like dogs, on trees and other natural landmarks. These areas may be as small as four square miles or as large as one thousand square miles. The size depends on the availability of prey, the climate, the type of terrain, and the presence of predators and other wolf packs. As Busch explains, "In the world of the wolf, a series of scent marks along a territory boundary constitutes an olfactory 'no trespassing' sign."[5] In addition to marking their hunting territory, wolves may also spray areas of recent kills to claim possession of the kill site.

Another form of marking territory is by leaving feces, or scat, behind. Wolves are known to leave scat every 250 yards along their most traveled hunting routes. Wolves also establish their presence in a territory by scratching. By pawing the ground, wolves are able to release odors from glands in their paws.

What's for dinner?

When food is plentiful, the average wolf will eat anywhere from five to twelve pounds of food a day. A full-grown wolf, however, can eat as much as twenty pounds of meat at one time. Wolves tend to eat whatever their environment offers. In addition to active hunting, wolves also scavenge for food.

In the tundra, wolves prefer caribou, but they have been known to eat mice, ground squirrels, and various birds. Red wolves tend to eat these smaller animals more often than the larger gray wolves. Raccoon and white-tailed deer are also a main staple in the red wolf's diet.

Wolf food selection changes with the seasons. In Canada, for example, gray wolves hunting alone in the summer months turn to beaver. When hunting in pack formation in the winter, they hunt game animals such as bison, caribou, deer, elk, moose, and musk oxen. While it is easier for wolves to hunt these larger animals as a pack, they are capable of killing them individually. Wolves also rely on fish as a year-round source of nourishment where fish are plentiful. Not all wolves, however, have the luxury of a varied food supply. In Ethiopia, for example, where there is much competition for food among packs, wolves live entirely off rodents.

Wolf senses

Wolves are aided in their hunting by their keen senses. While their capabilities of sight and hearing are impressive, by far the most

While wolves may travel great distances during a hunt, they tend to stay within the territory they have marked for themselves.

developed sense in wolves is that of smell. Wolf researcher David Mech explains that a wolf's sense of smell is up to one hundred times more sensitive than a human's; he has studied wolves that were able to pick up the scent of a moose over four miles away. A wolf's daytime vision is similar to a human's, but its nighttime vision is superior. Wolves' peripheral, or side, vision is also excellent, and they have a keen ability to detect moving objects. Able to detect sounds out of human range, wolves also have a sharp sense of hearing. Mech notes that "wolves can hear as far as six miles away in the forest and ten miles away on the open tundra."[6]

Howling it up

The wolf's heightened sense of hearing also helps it to communicate with other wolves. This communication takes the form of howling. Wolf howls range in duration from

After hunting as a pack during the winter, these gray wolves in the Boreal Forest in Canada are feasting on a recent kill, probably a game animal such as a deer or caribou.

Howling is an important method of communication for wolves. Different howls can designate location, call others to attention, or indicate an individual wolf's feelings of aggression, sadness, or elation.

half a second to eleven seconds. A group howl generally begins as barks from a few pack members, gradually changes to a low howl, then escalates into a loud packwide howl. All members of the wolf pack participate in howling behaviors, even the pups as young as a couple of months. Wolves howl most frequently in the evening and early morning during the winter or when breeding.

Wolves howl for a variety of reasons. One is to signal their pack location to other packs that may be passing within their territory, or to signal their hunting position to wolves within their pack. In order to sound more intimidating to possible intruders, each wolf in the pack howls at a different tone. This gives the impression that the wolf pack is large even if it is relatively small. In addition to howling to protect their territory, author Jim Brandenburg writes, wolves often howl after sleeping for long periods of time, and they howl to "work up the group into enthusiasm for the next hunt."[7]

Just as there are a variety of reasons to howl, there are different types of howls. Many researchers have noted that just as humans employ various inflections of voice to communicate through language, wolves howl for notably different lengths of time, and at different pitches, to communicate different messages. Author Lois Crisler writes that wolves may employ a "happy social howl, the mourning howl, the wild deep hunting howl, or the call howl,"[8] depending on the circumstances.

Keeping clean

In addition to making their howling music together and hunting as a group, wolves help each other keep clean. Busch explains that grooming each other helps "reinforce the social bonds that tie the pack together. Two wolves will lick each other's coats, nibbling gently with their teeth to remove foreign matter." Wolves that have been wounded receive special grooming attention from other pack members, an act, Busch says, that provides "both physical and mental comfort."[9]

Wolves are also conscious of grooming individually. Brandenburg says that the Arctic wolves he observed paid special attention to cleanliness, as their pure white coats provide them with camouflage against the winter snow. He recounts an incident in which one wolf, nicknamed "Buster," ended up covered in mud during his pursuit of a hare.

> Rather than lying down immediately to enjoy his meal, he took a long, careful swim, after which he shook himself dry—all with the dead hare clamped in his jaw. Only then did he sit down to his meal.[10]

Grooming is a social activity for wolves. These wolves are keeping clean by licking and nibbling each other's thick coats.

Dating and mating

Reproduction is another important wolf pack activity. Wolves only mate once a year within their packs, and typically only one male and female wolf mate during the breeding season. According to author Candace Savage, "94 percent of wild wolf packs produce only one litter per year, and . . . nearly 40 percent of mature females fail to reproduce each season."[11] Wolf packs, therefore, do not bring large numbers of pups into the wild each year.

With few pups to take the place of wolves that may die at any given time, it is understandable how harsh winters that limit food supply, or other threats outside of the pack, can negatively affect wolf populations. Sometimes, however, more wolf pups are born than usual. For instance, the natural social order of a pack may break down, especially if it is disrupted by the death of one of the alpha wolves. In these cases, more females are likely to produce litters for the pack.

Under normal conditions, however, as winter comes to a close, the dominant male and female wolves in the pack begin a courtship process that leads to breeding. Robert Busch describes the early stages of courtship as "flirting." The wolf pairs will "approach each other while making quiet whining sounds," he says. They will "mouth each other's muzzles, touch noses, and bump their bodies together."[12] Other courting behaviors include grooming each other's coats and nibbling on each other.

The courting wolves will mate anytime between January and April. Wolves are thought to pair and mate for life, and both parents look after their pups. Before the pups are born, however, the female wolf finds an underground den to use as her birthing chamber. The den consists of a long, narrow tunnel with a small hollow room at the end, large enough for the female wolf and her expected litter. If a ready-made den, such as one vacated by a fox or other animal, is not available, the female wolf may dig her own in the hillside, reside in the space between rocks, or find some other suitable natural enclosure in her surroundings.

In the spring, after a 59- to 63-day gestation period, generally four to seven wolf pups are born to the dominant pair. The female wolf protects the pups in her den while the male wolf collects food for her. Other pack members often wait at the den entrance whining in apparent anticipation of the pups' arrival outside the den. During her nursing period, the mother wolf is recognized as the supreme ruler of the pack. All of her actions, as well as the actions of other pack members, revolve around the needs of the new pups.

David Mech tested a female's control over food supply during this early pup-rearing period. Mech shot two Arctic hares for his test and tried to give one of them to the domi-

These Alaskan gray wolf pups will remain in their mother's underground den up to three months before exploring the outside world.

nant male of the pack in the presence of the nursing female. "He eagerly grabbed it," Mech says. "Instantly, however, the female sprang over to him, snatched the carcass out of his mouth, and took it a few hundred yards to the den and ate it."[13] With the female thus fed and apparently satisfied, Mech wondered if the male wolf would eat the second hare on his own. He did not. Instead, he proved his mate's temporary domination over him by eating only the head of the rabbit. He then brought the remainder of the rabbit over to the female, who carried it off and buried it.

Wolf pups are as playful and curious as domestic puppies. Unlike a dog, however, this pup will join its adult counterparts and begin hunting for food before it reaches a year old.

Pup meets world

When they are adequately supplied with food, wolf pups grow quickly. As they grow and the den quarters become cramped, the female wolf often moves the litter into a larger space. At two months old, the pups are ready to eat meat that is regurgitated for them by their parent wolves and other pack members. At three months, the wolf pups are stable enough to sleep outside the den. At six months, they look much like their adult counterparts. By winter they are ready to hunt with the rest of the pack.

Wolf pups are capable of breeding in their second year, but studies show that less than half the pups usually make it to adulthood. Depending on conditions of disease and malnutrition within the wolf pack, up to 80 percent of newborns do not survive their first year.

Those wolves that do survive most often leave their birth packs to try to form packs of their own. Within these packs they will form new social hierarchies and maintain their role of predators in the wild. Some will roam freely within their vast territories, hunting and reproducing without ever coming into contact with humans. Others may live in territory shrunken by habitat destruction, or they may become casualties of human fear and hatred.

2

The Great Hunter

WOLVES SURVIVE BY preying on other animals. Everything about wolves, from their natural instincts to their body structure and keen senses, helps them play their role of predator in the wild. Sometimes wolves' predatory nature may have a positive effect on the environment and on the continuation or control of other species, but the wolf's need to hunt has not always coincided with the specific goals of humans.

Quite possibly, then, the cause of the greatest threat to wolves is this need to hunt. The wolf has been seen as the enemy of hunters, who seek the same big game animals that wolves eat to survive, and ranchers, who fear wolf populations as a threat to their valuable cattle, sheep, and other domestic animals. In an effort to protect their own livelihoods, many people have responded to the potential threat of wolves by working to exterminate them in the wild.

Studies of wolves suggest that this response is an exaggerated one fueled by continuing fears and misconceptions about wolves. While wolves do hunt big game animals, and they do sometimes prey on ranchers' livestock, the damage they do does not seem to warrant calling for their total elimination. Simply understanding the wolf's hunting routine in the wild and the potential benefits of the wolf's predatory role in the environment can do much to ease some of the fears that have threatened wolf populations.

On the hunt

While nearly 50 percent of their day is spent in relative inactivity, wolves spend most of the rest of their time hunting for prey. When the pack hunts, it travels the same hunting route within its territory, sometimes traveling as far as sixty miles a day depending on the availability of food. After they make a large kill, however, wolves are known to lie around their campsites and return to resting and sleeping for days. When they set out to hunt again, several days may pass before they are able to find prey and make another kill.

Wolf packs often band together to capture large prey to increase their chances of having a successful hunt. During the hunt, wolves chase packs of wild game and try to separate the youngest and weakest animals from the group. Once the targeted prey is separated, the wolf pack surrounds it on all sides and tears at its flesh until it is dead. The wolves then usually eat the carcass immediately, although sometimes they leave behind portions of their kills for later.

Waste not, want not

In instances when wolves do not consume their entire kill, they are likely to bury large portions of meat in the snow or elsewhere underground. This behavior is known as

Wolves are known to devour most of what they kill. Meat that is left behind, however, helps feed foxes, squirrels, birds, and other scavengers in the environment.

caching. Cached meat that survives scavengers is dug up and eaten when the wolves return to the kill. Little is known about the conditions under which caching occurs. It confirms the view of most experts, however, that wolves eventually eat nearly every part of their kills.

During his observations on Isle Royale in Lake Superior, researcher David Mech found that all of fifty moose carcasses he examined were eventually eaten completely. Other researchers in Alaska found that two-thirds of thirty-one caribou and moose kills were 75 percent eaten, and 72 percent of deer carcasses in Ontario, Canada, were also 75 percent utilized.

Author Rick Bass describes wolves as "deadly serious about the business of surviving in the world—and yet they are not excessive" in their hunting.

> There is in them some natural restraint, and in pulling up just shy of greed, not crossing that last line at which wastefulness begins, they have gained as a species a certain kind of strength. We can't measure it, we can't even articulate it, but it exists. There is no other word for it other than spirit.[14]

A little help from nature

In addition to caching, the wolf's anatomy also helps contribute to survival in the wild. As noted, the wolf's large stomach capacity allows it to eat large amounts of food. A single wolf, for example, can consume twenty pounds of meat in one feeding. This food supply keeps wolves alive during times when food is scarce.

The wolf's bone structure also aids in successful hunting. Wolves have long limbs made up of slender bones. Walking on their digits, rather than the soles of their feet, they are able to reach speeds of up to thirty miles per hour. Their lack of a collarbone gives them a wide range of motion when running or jumping, and their nonretractable claws help them to grip onto loose surfaces.

When hunting in the winter, wolves are further aided in their chasing of prey by the pads on the bottom of their feet. These pads, surrounded by thick hair for extra warmth, help wolves grip the ice when they are traveling across frozen

areas. Because wolves are light enough to run on top of snow often without falling through, they use this to their advantage in chasing large game animals. Wolves have been known to chase big animals into deep snow, where their movements are slowed and they are unable to escape.

The fur-edged pads on the bottom of this gray wolf's feet help keep it warm as it travels across the snow-covered landscape.

Going hungry

Despite their image as ferocious killers, wolves are not always successful hunters. A strong, healthy moose, for example, can survive a wolf attack simply by standing its ground. While following a wolf pack for a full hunting season on Isle Royale in 1960, Mech recorded seventy-seven moose kill attempts and only six successes.

Mech concludes that wolves generally have a low hunting-success rate. He says that an animal that does get preyed upon by wolves is usually one that is surprised by wolves. Perhaps it is in a situation where it is surrounded by wolves and its escape route is cut off. Other animals may be psychologically inferior, meaning they do not have the wits to escape an aggressive situation, or they may be behaviorally inferior, having a poor sense of sight, hearing, or smell. Newborn animals and those that are malformed, sick, old, wounded, or otherwise disadvantaged are also prime targets of wolves.

The reason wolves have a difficult time capturing prey in its prime is that nature has equipped these species with their own detection and defense systems against predators. When these systems are working well, Mech says, these animals are unlikely to fall victim to wolf kills. If these systems are defective or not fully developed, wolves and other predators take advantage of these prey for means of survival.

The wolf's predatory role in the environment

Wolf predation of already weakened or diseased animals is actually beneficial to the biosphere. This removal of biologically inferior animals has been called the "sanitation effect" by modern biologists. When wolves prey on diseased animals they are, in effect, cleansing disease from the prey species. Killing a diseased deer, for example, prevents the disease from spreading throughout the rest of the herd. While wounded or crippled animals are not necessarily as harmful to their herds as diseased animals, predation of diseased and injured animals contributes to the efficiency of the herd, as these members are less likely to survive long enough to reproduce.

This "sanitation" system of hunting is common in nature. As Rick Bass explains,

> The wolf pack exploits irregularities within the natural system in order to take what the system—the woods, the prairie, the desert, the mountains—has to offer. If a deer herd expands excessively, the wolves bear down on it. Ten deer run from the packs' approach. Over time the slowest deer are the ones that are caught most often, the ones that stumble are fallen upon. The vigor of the herd is protected, even enhanced.[15]

In addition to contributing to the "sanitation" of other species, there is evidence that wolf hunting practices actually contribute to the management of some species. David Mech experienced this firsthand when he followed one wolf pack in Minnesota. This pack "varied its killing by hunting in a different part of its territory each year, allowing prey numbers elsewhere to recover, aiding the long-term survival of the pack."[16] In this case, the wolves were able to survive from year to year without eliminating such large populations of their prey that both species would be negatively affected.

Wolf kills (and all predators' kills) thus help keep some populations of species in the wild in check. They also indirectly help other species to survive. The "chain of events that might result from wolf predation on a moose are as follows," Mech says:

> (1) Where the moose falls, its blood, hair, bones, and stomach contents slowly disintegrate and add their minerals and humus to the soil, (2) as a result, the general area of the kill becomes more fertile and eventually supports a lush stand of small herbs and shrubs, (3) a litter of snowshoe hares pays frequent visits to the area to feed on the nutritious plants, (4) the presence of the hares draws foxes and other predators, and incidentally these remove many of the mice that live nearby, (5) a weasel that used to hunt these mice then shifts its activities to another area, and in doing so falls prey to an owl.[17]

Wolf kills are beneficial to a number of other animals in the wild, especially those that are poorly adapted for killing

"Well, if—as everyone insists—we've a superior organisation, communications system, ecological sense and an ability to adjust, how is it we're becoming extinct?"

animals themselves. These scavengers feed on what little remains of animals wolves do leave behind. Scavengers include birds such as eagles, ravens, and vultures, as well as part-time scavengers like foxes, squirrels, coyotes, bobcats, and even bears.

For an area of land to be able to support a variety of scavenger animals, food must be available to them year-round. "Because wolf predation provides a relatively stable quantity of food throughout the year, it probably allows an area to support higher numbers of scavengers than other mortality factors [such as starvation and disease of game animals] would,"[18] Mech says.

Tipping the scales

Although wolves are often thought of as insatiable killers, they hunt only as much prey as they need to survive. Wolves also do not reproduce often enough to place prey species in danger of extinction.

Due to a number of natural processes, such as territorial limits and social interactions among the pack, wolves generally do not reproduce quickly enough to diminish their food supply. "Over the long term and over large areas, wolves and their prey both manage to get by,"[19] says Candace Savage. Occasionally, however, wolves do tip the balance in nature and can damage the population of their prey species.

In the early 1970s, for example, Isle Royale suffered a number of severe winters that caused extensive damage to the environment and many of the animal species on the island. "Mired in deep snow, half-starved and weak, adult and calf moose both became easy pickings for a large and energetic population of wolves,"[20] Savage says. The result was that the moose population on Isle Royale was cut in half by the middle of the 1970s. However, the wolf population continued to grow to three times its original size by 1980.

"Apparently," Savage says, "the calves that had grown up during hard times remained vulnerable to predation throughout their lifetimes, so the wolves continued to feast even after the moose had tottered into decline." Nature, however, soon readjusted itself. As Savage notes:

> Eventually, through a gruesome combination of malnutrition, social strife and disease, the wolves were also reduced from a triumphant high of fifty to a remnant of fourteen individuals. Since then, although moose populations have recovered fully, the fortunes of the wolves have been uncertain. For reasons that remain obscure (inbreeding? illness?), they have rebounded and died off, rebounded and died off, and rebounded again, in a wavering struggle against extinction.[21]

The battle between wolves and ranchers

If wolves stayed within their territories, preying on animals that do not belong to anyone, it is unlikely that wolves would ever be hunted for predation prevention. Wolves do not understand the boundary lines between the wilderness and a private ranch or other property, however. They wander outside these boundaries, especially if their food source in their regular territory has vanished because of drought, a harsh winter, or some other reason. In this case, wolves will wander farther than usual in their hunt for food. If they come across a calf on this hunt, they will surely eat it.

Therefore, it is natural for ranchers to be concerned about wolves that may pose an immediate menace to their livestock. Research suggests, however, that wolves pose less of a threat to livestock than ranchers believe. In Montana, for instance, between 1987 and 1995, wolves killed

During harsh winters or times of drought, wolves are more likely to prey on ranchers' livestock as they wander outside their usual territory in search of food.

twenty-four cattle and twelve sheep. Given the number of cattle and sheep roaming Montana ranch land, thirty-six livestock losses in six years represents only a tiny percentage. Statistics from research in other states seem to concur in this finding. According to the Defenders of Wildlife organization, for instance, "in Minnesota where the wolf population is 1,700, the level of predation amounts to about one-hundredth of 1 percent of the local cattle, and one-fourth of 1 percent of the nearby sheep. Thousands of times more sheep are killed by pet dogs than by wolves."[22]

One rancher told author Peter Steinhart that if the wolves just stayed up in the hills, things would be fine by him. However, he says,

> Some of the people here are much more shoot-'em-on-sight people. As long as they don't bother me, I've got no problem with 'em. I could live with 'em. It's just another hazard. But if they're out here killing cows, and I've got my rifle, if I can kill them, I would.[23]

Bruce Thisted, a rancher in Montana whose small valley has become a rendezvous spot for a pack of wolves, tolerates the presence of wolves, but he feels sure the wolves will "get into trouble sooner or later. Anything that's found dead," he says, "the wolves are just going to get blamed for it. Years ago, a farmer would lose a cow and he'd drag it out on the railroad track [and blame the railroad for the loss]. It's going to be the same with the wolves: if they lose a cow, they'll blame it on wolves."[24]

Farmers on the East Coast, where there is a proposal for wolves to be returned to the Adirondacks and parts of Maine and New Hampshire, share the concerns of western ranchers. Mark F. Emery, a spokesman for the New York Farm Bureau, speaks out against wolves, pointing to the fact that there is no way to police wolves so that they remain within the boundaries of Adirondack Park. "We already have an overabundance of predators, particularly coyotes," Emery says. "From a livestock standpoint, the wolf would do a number on sheep operations and also dairy farms. There are both sheep and dairy operations in the park itself and within a short distance."[25]

Wolves in hunters' territory

Like ranchers, hunters foster some resentment of the wolf's predatory nature. A common concern of sport hunters is the competition the wolf presents for prey, such as deer, elk, moose, and bison, that they seek themselves as trophies. Robert McClung writes that many hunters "still think of any and all predators as outlaws that kill game that belongs—by some divine right—to the human hunter."[26]

Many hunters support wolf extermination programs because wolves prey on the same game animals that hunters seek for themselves.

While it seems logical to conclude that fewer wolves means more prey for human hunters, it is not clear if the wolf is really a *significant* competitor with humans for these animals. Most areas that wolves inhabit are remote and often inaccessible, and few hunters ever venture into them. For this reason, Mech believes it is "not accurate to state that wolves actually had been competing with hunters to any significant degree."[27]

Like ranchers, hunters' fears about wolf predation do not always take into account the reality of the big game situation. Ted Koch, who leads the U.S. Fish and Wildlife Service's Wolf Recovery Project in Idaho, says, for instance, "Hunters say they don't want wolves killing their elk, but poachers kill at least five times as much elk as a full pack of wolves."[28]

Although wolves do prey on elk and deer and other game, game animal numbers have not declined as a result. Deer populations have even increased in the lower forty-eight states despite wolf inhabitance over the past two decades. In Wisconsin, the deer population increased from 605,000 in 1963 to 1 million in 1993. In Minnesota, annual deer harvests rose from 67,106 animals in 1973 to 188,109 animals in 1993, despite the fact that the wolf population grew from less than 1,000 to almost 2,000.

Hunters worry not only about wolf predation but also about their own access to areas that contain protected wolf populations. Hunters fear that because wolves are a protected species, wildlife agencies will not sell hunting licenses in wolf territory. Hunting license sales, however, do not seem to have been affected. In Minnesota alone, hunting license sales increased from 325,405 to 559,808 from 1973 to 1993. These facts should be encouraging to hunters, but they are still wary of the wolf's presence.

Finding the middle ground

Ranchers and hunters, as well as environmentalists, have often exaggerated their arguments for or against the existence of wolves in the wild. Renee Askins, executive director of Wolf Fund, an environmental organization in Moose,

Wyoming, believes that the truth of the wolf issue lies somewhere in the middle of these different claims.

"Wolves are not killing machines that deserve hideous deaths," she says; "neither are they cuddly creatures needing tender, righteous protection. Wolves survive by killing; they have an extraordinary and complex social system; they are smart, strong, and at the core, consummate predators. Restoring wolves will not rescue us from our economic or ecological troubles, but neither will their presence contribute to them." Ranchers, Askins concludes, will always lose some sheep and cattle to wolves, and hunters will have a few less game animals to hunt. Neither hunters nor ranchers, however, will "face economic doom due to the presence of wolves."[29]

3

Wolf as Prey

THROUGHOUT HISTORY, THE wolf has been subjected to acts of cruelty and extermination campaigns. Often these actions were sanctioned by the government, which sought to control wolf predation of livestock and big game animals. These control efforts included wolf bounty programs, which paid hunters fees for each wolf killed, and organized wolf kills, in which wolves were killed on a mass scale.

Bounty programs and organized wolf kills have contributed greatly to the endangerment and, in some cases, extinction of wolves in the United States and elsewhere. Today these programs are no longer legal where wolves are protected under the Endangered Species Act. However, wolf elimination programs are still sometimes carried out in Alaska and Canada, both of which have thriving wolf populations.

Bounties on the wolf

Wolves in North America were transformed from hunter to hunted in significant numbers beginning in the 1600s. The settlers of the original U.S. colonies introduced sheep and other livestock to North America in 1512. Cattle, horses, and pigs arrived from Europe later in 1609. The open pastures that the settlers created for their livestock made the animals easy targets for wolves whose natural prey, deer, had been steadily diminished because of the settlers' hunting of them. As a result, the first American wolf bounty was instituted in Massachusetts in 1630.

As settlers traveled west, they severely depleted most populations of bison, deer, elk, and moose. These big game animals were important prey for wolves. When their numbers dwindled, the western wolf, like its eastern counterpart, turned to the settlers' sheep and cattle that had replaced its

In this 1821 illustration, a man on a rooftop shoots at a pack of wolves. The picture depicts the human fear and loathing of wolves that led to wolf bounties and extermination programs.

natural prey. To protect their livestock, ranchers and government agencies campaigned to eliminate the wolf.

During the 1860s and 1870s, western ranchers invested large amounts of money in cattle, as the arrival of the railroad introduced new markets to them. Many ranchers, however, lost cattle to severe droughts. Also suffering from the droughts, wolves in search of food preyed on cattle herds more frequently, which contributed to ranchers' losses. When "drought recurrently decimated these herds," Peter Steinhart writes, "ranchers looked to trim what adversities they could. There was not a thing they could do about the weather. But they could do something about predators."[30] The result? Many ranchers hired men as "wolfers" (wolf hunters) to eliminate the wolf population.

A war of sorts was thus waged against the wolf as more states set up bounty payments for wolves and bounty hunters used any means necessary to catch their prey. Wolfers bought wagon loads of strychnine, for example.

This Canadian trapper of the 1920s worked at a time when wolf pelts were in great demand for use as ladies' fur coats, parkas, and other products.

"Anywhere a cowhand found a dead cow or deer or dog, he would get down from his horse and lace the meat with poison," Steinhart writes. Should wolves happen to eat the poisoned meat, they would be killed and could then be turned in for bounty money. Cruelty toward wolves became commonplace. "Cowboys roped wolves, strung them between horses, and spurred the horse until the wolves were torn apart. They doused them with gasoline and set them on fire,"[31] Steinhart writes.

The efforts of U.S. bounty hunters greatly contributed to the eventual endangerment of wolves. Within the first thirty-five years of Montana's bounty program alone, more than eighty thousand wolves were killed. In Wyoming, more than thirty-six thousand were killed between 1895 and 1917.

Bounty programs initiated in the nineteenth century continued as late as 1967. In 1960, thirty-three states paid out more than $2 million in bounties on predators such as wolves. In 1966, Alaska paid a $50 bounty for each of the thirteen hundred wolves killed there. Under these modern bounty programs, wolves, like their ancestors, were not always killed in a humane fashion. They were trapped in devices that caused slow deaths, were shot from planes and snowmobiles, and also hunted with dogs. In 1967, McClung writes, "Private 'sportsman's' single engine planes were permitted to pursue wolves until the animals were exhausted, then land and shoot them."[32]

Government votes to exterminate the wolf

In addition to bounty programs, various mass extermination programs helped cause widespread extinction or endangerment of wolves in the United States. In 1915, American ranchers convinced the government to participate in a national campaign to eliminate wolves. Under the Predator and Rodent Control (PARC) section of the Bureau of Biological Survey, government employees and hunters together killed off most of the wolf populations living in the lower forty-eight states. Wolves, including El Lobo, the Mexican wolf, were eliminated in Texas by 1925 and in Arizona by 1926.

Shortly after that, in 1931, Congress enacted the Animal Damage Control Act. This act gave the U.S. Department of Agriculture the funds and authority to kill predatory species deemed a threat to people, livestock, and wild game. Numerous animals, including the wolf, were identified in this law as dangerous predators. Under this act, wolves did not have to be caught in the act of predation to be deemed threatening. A wolf's passing through a populated area was enough for it to be seen as a potential menace.

In response to this legislation, the government later authorized the use of sodium monofluoroacetate (a chemical created by the army to kill rats in Southeast Asia) for predator control in the 1940s. Eventually named Compound 1080, the odorless, tasteless substance could be easily injected into dead animals that wolves would be likely to feed on, and the poison would stay potent for months. This chemical "predacide"—so called because it was used to kill predators—allowed predator control programs to cover vast areas with less manpower than it would take to seek out and kill wolves individually.

The Animal Damage Control Act has continued to affect wolves in recent decades. In 1989, for example, eighty wolves were killed under the act. And in 1993 the Animal Damage Control unit still had "an annual budget of $30 million or more, and more than six hundred employees who shoot, trap, and poison such predators throughout the country,"[33] says Robert McClung.

Hunting wolves to save big game populations

Organized, government-sponsored wolf kills and various predator control programs were set up not only to protect livestock from wolf predation, but also to protect wild game. The reasons are both environmental and monetary. If wolf predation of elk in a specific region is greater than normal and the elk population is threatened, agents will take steps to reduce the number of wolves in the area, thereby saving the elk. Often, however, when big game numbers are down, wolves are targeted, based on the fear of and misconceptions about wolves rather than their actual role in the dwindling numbers of a specific species.

In some instances, wolf control programs are set up not to protect a dwindling population of game but to assure sufficient numbers of wild game for hunters. Through their purchasing of hunting licenses and payment of admission fees to hunting areas, hunters bring in revenue to states. Wildlife officers are not likely to eliminate their wolf control programs because they are "challenged to provide bountiful hunting for their clientele,"[34] Candace Savage says.

Large-scale organized wolf kills have been carried out in Canada and Alaska. Wolves are abundant in both regions, and wildlife officials often voice their concerns over the wolves' potential impact on big game populations. Plans

A Forest Service hunter rides with a wolf slung across his saddle in Colorado's White River National Forest in 1923.

for these wolf kills, however, are often met with public opposition. In Canada in 1983, for example, the British Columbia Wildlife Branch planned to kill 80 percent of the wolves in the two northeast districts of Peace and Omineca. Stating that the wolf kill would help to save the declining moose and deer populations, the government organized a public lottery to help pay for the wolf elimination campaign.

One government report, however, stated that game populations had not decreased because of wolves but because of habitat loss, overhunting, and severe winters. Canadian wildlife biologists also stated, "There is no biological basis or biological justification for the wolf control program."[35] When the Canadian public learned that there was no true biological need for the program, they voiced their anger and the government called off the hunt. More than four hundred wolves were killed, however, before the elimination program was discontinued.

Similarly, in 1993, the Canadian government made plans to kill 150 wolves near the Kluane National Park in the Yukon, with the hope of supporting a declining caribou herd. The government felt that removing the threat of wolves would give the caribou population a chance to replenish itself. Though the World Wildlife Fund of Canada and other organizations discovered that this kill was also biologically unjustified, the program went forward as planned.

Canadian gray wolves, like this one, make up the largest population of wolves in the world. Large-scale wolf hunts are still carried out in Canada to limit wolf predation of game animals.

Later, under public pressure, the government stated that the elimination program was more a "scientific experiment" than a case of predation control (although in what sense it was scientific is unclear). After additional probing, biologists also found that the population of wolves in the kill area was 40 percent smaller than originally estimated. This finding suggests that wolves could not have been responsible for as much of the predation on the caribou herd as they were blamed for. The government, however, did not call off the program.

Organized wolf kills in Alaska

In Alaska, the wolf population currently remains about seven thousand, and wolves are not protected as an endangered species. As in Canada, however, McClung notes that Alaskan wolves are still "frequently made scapegoats for any decline of caribou, moose, deer, or mountain sheep populations, despite a great deal of wildlife research to the contrary." [36]

Over the past three decades, Alaska has permitted aerial hunting as both a means of culling the wolf population and for sport. The most recent organized wolf control program, in 1992, was scheduled in response to a decline of the Delta caribou. The planned hunt called for killing three hundred to four hundred wolves the first year and one hundred to three hundred wolves annually thereafter. As wolves often feed on Delta caribou, wildlife officials hoped that reducing the number of wolves would help the herd recover. In this case, however, a biologist with Alaska's Department of Fish and Game publicly stated that declines in the Delta herd were likely due to nutritional stress and other environmental conditions, not from wolves.

Aerial hunting of wolves, and mass extermination programs in general, has been criticized in public opinion polls in Alaska. Hoping to prevent the scheduled 1992–1993 hunt, the Defenders of Wildlife and other conservation groups initiated a boycott against Alaska's tourist industry. More than forty thousand citizens also petitioned against the hunt. These actions led to a scaling down of the planned killing and, later in 1993, a ban on aerial hunting. The ban on aerial hunting, however, does not prevent wolves from being hunted. In fact, with a $15 "trapping" license, private citizens are still allowed to *track* wolves from the air, land, and then shoot them, provided hunters move one hundred feet from the plane before doing so. This practice has invariably contributed to the high number of wolf kills in the 1990s. During the winter of 1993–1994, for example, a twenty-year wolf mortality record was broken in Alaska when an estimated 1,572 wolves were killed.

Some biologists, such as Bob Stephenson from the Alaskan Department of Fish and Game, feel that aerial wolf hunts should continue as an option for wolf control when needed. Stephenson believes that aerial hunting is more "efficient and economical, and arguably more humane, than ground-based control methods [hunting and shooting or trapping wolves on foot]. If you have to do predator control," he says, "why handicap yourself? I don't see traps and snares as better for the wolves. Aerial control is a saner way to do it."[37]

Stephenson says that the aerial ban also increases animosity between rural Alaskan hunters and what they describe as "urban, politically correct, holier-than-thou environmentalists." He explains:

> It's easy to say "leave the wolves alone" if you live in the city. But if you're a rural resident who's dependent on wild game, there may be times when your food source is threatened by high wolf numbers. The fact is wolves are a major player in Alaska's ecosystems: there are places where they have a whole lot to do with wildlife abundance. You can't ignore local people or there's going to be a backlash. If there's no management, locals will take matters into their own hands.[38]

Hunting wolves for pelts and sport

Wolves are not only killed for predator control measures. They are also hunted for the fur trade. Like bears and moose, they are hunted by sportsmen as big game animals, their pelts preserved as personal trophies.

Wolf pelts are the most traded part of wolves and are most often used for parka trim. Many fur trappers, however, have turned away from wolf pelts because the cost of preparing the pelts for market often exceeds their value. Today in Canada, with a wolf population of twenty-five thousand or more, three thousand pelts are taken yearly for the fur trade. In the 1920s, however, when wolf pelts were at their greatest demand, wolf trapping was more popular. Between 1927 and 1928, for instance, over twenty-one thousand wolves were killed for the fur trade.

In the United States, wolf trapping is legal only in Alaska, where the wolf is not endangered. Although there is no limit to the number of wolves trappers can take there, trapping kills remain relatively low. During the 1992–1993 trapping season, trappers killed only 344 wolves.

Wolf hunting was established as a sport in Europe as early as the sixteenth century, and it gained popularity in North America during the 1800s. Dogs known as wolf-hounds were bred for the sport, and in Asia, even eagles were used as aids in the hunt. As in the case of trapping, hunting wolves for sport in America only remains legal in

Some hunters kill wolves to keep their beautiful pelts as trophies. In the United States, however, trapping and hunting wolves for sport is legal only in Alaska.

Alaska. Popular since the 1960s, the most common method of hunting wolves for sport in Alaska is by snowmobile. The hunting season lasts from August through April, and hunters are limited to two to ten wolves each depending on the location.

Fewer wolves are killed each year by trappers and sportsmen than by predator control programs, and in areas where wolves are plentiful, these killings do not add significantly to potential endangerment. In regions that have very small wolf populations, however, if wolves were not protected by the Endangered Species Act (ESA), the smallest amount of sports hunting or trapping could very easily lead to extinction. Thus these activities are strictly regulated by the ESA.

Decades of bounty and predator control programs have nearly succeeded in eliminating the wolf from the American landscape. Many citizens have worked to halt the wolf's decline, but it is too soon to know whether those efforts will succeed.

4

Habitat Destruction and the Search for New Homes

EXTERMINATION PROGRAMS, HUNTING, and trapping are not the only causes of wolf endangerment. Wolves need room to roam and access to prey in the wild. A typical pack may require territory ranging anywhere from eighteen square miles to one thousand square miles, depending on hunting conditions. Therefore, when their habitat is disrupted, for whatever reason, their existence may become threatened.

While natural disasters such as floods, drought, and harsh winters may force wolves to seek new territories and may affect population numbers, it is most often human actions that destroy crucial wolf habitat. The clearing of trees for the development of homes, industries, roads, and other human needs has reduced available living area for wolves. Habitats have also been lost to pollution caused by chemical or industrial waste.

In response to the destruction of wolf habitats, environmental groups and wildlife biologists have worked to secure places where wolves can live in relative peace. National parks play a big role in providing protected territory for wolves that is comparable to their natural habitats. Special wolf parks offer limited and controlled numbers of wolves security in natural settings as well. Traditional zoos also provide safe living environments and participate in captive breeding programs that are essential for the preservation of some wolf species. A final alternative, though less formal and less controlled than the others, is found in the adoption of wolves as pets.

If wolves are to be saved from extinction, their habitat needs to be large enough so that they may roam without human interference. Author Rick Bass believes it would be useless to restore wolves in the wild if plans are not first made to protect their habitat. "We will need wilderness, big wilderness, little wilderness, and in-between wilderness. Wilderness is not a renewable resource. It is finite and it is dwindling each year." Without this wilderness, Bass claims, wolves may become "some lesser, subdued species." [39]

The red wolf

Canis rufus, or the red wolf, was declared an endangered species in 1967 and became extinct in the wild in 1980. Habitat destruction played a key role in the red wolf's extinction. Originally, the red wolf could be found from Texas to Florida and in northern forested regions of North Carolina, Kentucky, Illinois, and Missouri. They roamed in areas of about twenty-five to fifty square miles that provided heavy vegetation. As more of its original habitat was destroyed, the red wolf adapted to life in southeastern coastal prairies and marshlands for a while but eventually its numbers dwindled.

Land clearing and drainage projects had a big impact on red wolf habitat in the early years of the twentieth century. Wolves that were not killed outright to make way for building projects had difficulty surviving the clearing of hardwood river bottoms that made up much of their habitat. In the Smoky Mountains of Tennessee, for example, the last red wolf was shot during land clearing projects in 1905.

As new roads were paved and the logging and mineral industries made their way into previous red wolf territory, those wolves that were not initially killed had difficulty adapting to their changing environment. Land clearing leveled hillsides that once provided space for mother wolves to dig birthing dens, and other naturally protective elements of the landscape, such as fallen trees or rocky crevices, were also cleared away. Land clearing also removed much of the vegetation and hence the small animals that fed on it, both of which red wolves relied on for survival. As a result of development projects, by 1970 fewer than eighty red wolves remained in the United States. They lived in small areas of coastal Texas and Louisiana. By the late 1970s only fourteen of these wolves were still alive; these were taken into captivity for protection.

The shrinking habitats of other animals, particularly the coyote, have also compromised the red wolf population. In eastern Texas and Oklahoma, for example, deforestation has destroyed coyote habitat. When the coyotes were forced to move farther eastward into red wolf territory, they had a direct impact on the already endangered wolf population. A shortage of mates for red wolves led to interbreeding

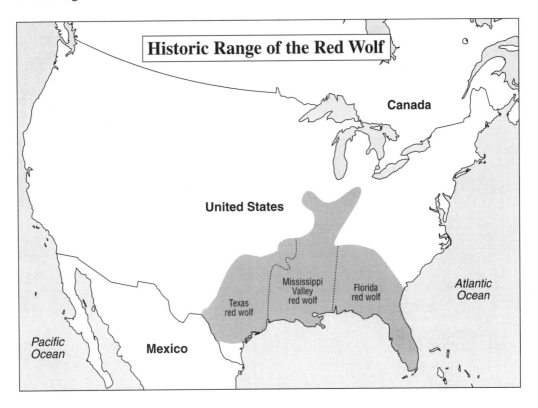

Historic Range of the Red Wolf

Habitat destruction contributed to the endangerment of the red wolf by forcing it to move outside its natural territory.

with the coyote population and sometimes even with stray dogs. This interbreeding lessened the genetic purity of red wolves and further contributed to the endangerment of the red wolf as a separate wolf species.

The rare Ethiopian wolf

Like the red wolf, the population of Ethiopian, or Abyssinian, wolves in Africa has declined to the brink of extinction due, in part, to habitat destruction. Currently, the

Ethiopian wolf, which lives in Ethiopia's high mountain enclaves, is recognized as one of the rarest canids in the world.

Ethiopian farmers who rely on high altitude farming for their own survival have directly affected Ethiopian wolf habitat by allowing their livestock to overgraze on lands that once supported wolves. Overgrazing by livestock depletes the supply of vegetation that provides nourishment to rodents such as mole rats and grass rats, which are the Ethiopian wolf's main source of food. Without vegetation, the rodent population diminishes, and without rodents, the wolves likewise go hungry.

Because of its shrinking range of habitat, the Ethiopian wolf is also forced to compete for food with domestic dogs. Like the red wolf, the Ethiopian wolf has interbred with local dogs, and thus has not only threatened its genetic purity, but also exposed itself to diseases, such as rabies and distemper, that were not originally found within the wolf population.

A bleak future

As a direct result of these challenges in its environment, the Ethiopian wolf suffers the highest mortality rate of any other wolf. Most Ethiopian wolves die by the age of one as a result of starvation or disease. By March 1992, for example, 41 wolves in the Bale Mountains had died of rabies. The adult Ethiopian wolf population numbered between 205 and 270 in 1992. An outbreak of distemper among domestic dogs reduced that number to between 120 and 160 surviving in 1997.

In addition to a shrinking food supply and the various threats resulting from mingling with dogs, the Ethiopian wolf's life has been endangered by civil war. In 1991, for example, civil unrest in the Bale Mountains led to the deaths of seven wolves and five pups. While twelve deaths would not have been significant in a healthy wolf population, for a small wolf population such as the Ethiopian wolf, every new death is closer to the extinction of the species.

Ethiopian wolf habitat was also directly affected by the civil war. Although the Ethiopian wolves once shared their habitat with the livestock of the moorland shepherds in the

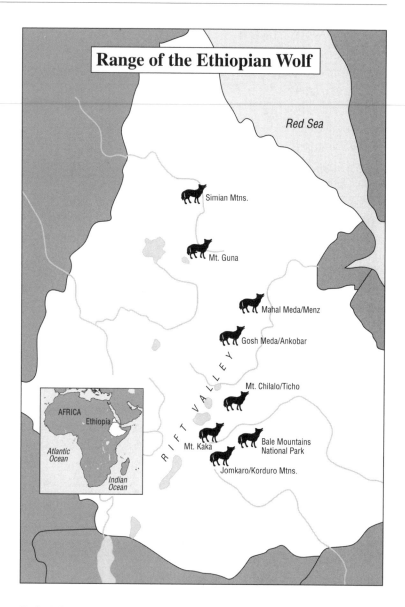

Range of the Ethiopian Wolf

Red Sea

Simian Mtns.

Mt. Guna

Mahal Meda/Menz

Gosh Meda/Ankobar

Mt. Chilalo/Ticho

RIFT VALLEY

Mt. Kaka

Bale Mountains
National Park

Jomkaro/Korduro Mtns.

AFRICA

Ethiopia

Atlantic
Ocean

Indian
Ocean

Bale Mountains, the farmers' increasing economic difficulties
led to increased land clearing for farming and overgrazing. As
a result, the Ethiopian wolves' habitat has steadily shrunk.

Finding a new home

Aware of the wolf's need for habitat protection, environmentalists and others concerned with the future of the wolf
have worked to conserve existing habitats and to counter-

act habitat loss by creating new homes for wolves that need them. In the United States, national parks, privately funded wolf parks, and traditional zoos have played a vital role in this habitat conservation.

National parks

National parks, such as Yellowstone in Wyoming, supply the most undisturbed land in the United States for protected wildlife. Such reserves help protect endangered species, such as wolves, because people are not allowed to hunt or build in them. More than 130 federally listed endangered species reside in national parks, including red and gray wolves.

The National Park Service considers a number of criteria when deciding which species are eligible for restoration within U.S. parks. In the case of wolves, the park must show that it has adequate habitat and ample natural resources to support a growing wolf population. Another concern for park management is the potential threat wolves may pose to park visitors, other species, or property outside of park boundaries. If this threat is judged insignificant when coupled with a wolf management plan, wolf restoration programs may begin. Finally, park officials look at the causes behind the wolves' disappearance. National parks sponsor wolf restoration only when biologists can prove that wolf endangerment in the region was a direct or indirect result of human interference with the wolves or their habitat.

When they do participate in species restoration projects, national parks do not just provide generic land for endangered animals; they maintain critical habitats that are specific to each species. Critical habitats include areas of land, from beaches to forests; water, such as swamps and estuaries; and even air space, needed for various species to breed, hunt, and relax in. The National Park System includes more than 360 parks that preserve habitats ranging from Arctic tundra to tropical rain forests. For wolves, national parks provide both the space and prey needed for wolves to maintain their natural pack activities.

In addition to providing wolves with adequate habitat, many national parks also participate in propagation programs. For example, on Horn Island, which is part of the Gulf Islands National Seashore off the Mississippi mainland, red wolves are bred in captivity but are still afforded the freedom to roam the island. When the mother wolf is ready to give birth, the adult pair on the island is placed in an acclimation pen. A few weeks after the pups are born, they are set free, along with the adults. When the pups further mature, they are captured and rereleased into the wild at other southeastern sites working to raise red wolf populations. The National Park Service writes that "such island propagation sites may ensure a continuing supply of healthy young wolves to the mainland population until recovery of the species is achieved."[40]

Wolf parks

Unlike national parks that may contain a variety of protected species, wolf parks, as their name suggests, cater specifically to wolves. Unwanted wolves, especially those born and raised as pets and then abandoned, often find homes through organizations that run wolf park sanctuaries. There are a variety of wolf parks in the United States and Europe, and while their first priority is providing wolves with a safe environment, wolf parks also work to educate the public and promote wolf conservation worldwide. Many wolf parks offer public tours of their facilities, and they also participate in wolf research and captive breeding programs.

Wolf Haven

One of the most well known wolf parks is Wolf Haven International, located in western Washington. Wolves that reside at Wolf Haven have most often been kept as pets previously and have been brought there by owners who have found raising a wolf too difficult to handle or care for once it reached maturity. Raised in a domestic setting, these wolves would have little chance of surviving in the wild. Although hunting is an instinctive behavior for wolves,

those raised in captivity would not have had the same opportunities as wild wolves to develop hunting skills. Captive wolves released in the wild also do not have the benefit of a pack to enhance their chances of survival.

The Wolf Haven sanctuary covers sixty-five acres and is home to thirty-nine wolves. Numerous trees and shrubs within the enclosure provide wolves with a natural environment and an opportunity to seek private shelter away from the park's visitors. The wolves are spayed or neutered to prevent them from breeding, as it is not the goal of Wolf Haven to increase its population of captive wolves.

In addition to providing support for once-captive wolves, Wolf Haven is working to develop programs that protect wolves in the wild. This goal has been accomplished in part by working closely with federal and state agencies and assisting with wolf recovery efforts in Washington, Montana, and Idaho. Under recovery programs, the population decline of endangered wolf species is reversed—most often through captive breeding programs that prepare wolves for release into the wild.

A gray wolf roams in the natural setting of its spacious pen at Wolf Haven wolf park in Washington State.

Public support for Wolf Haven and similar programs suggests that American citizens care about endangered wolves and their need for protected habitat. As of 1997, Wolf Haven has more than twenty-six thousand members and has an annual budget of nearly $1 million. Wolf Haven is not only concerned with promoting wolf conservation in the United States, however; the organization also plans to work with governments and other environmental organizations in Europe, Mexico, and the former Soviet Union.

Wolf Haven has already made a start in that direction. In 1996, the organization embarked on a Mexican wolf recovery program. The Mexican wolves that now reside in Wolf Haven's breeding facility signify a new era for Wolf Haven: captive breeding of rare wolves for eventual release in the wild. As its Mexican wolf program is still in its beginning stages, Wolf Haven has not yet released any into the wild.

Lastly, Wolf Haven has also made a commitment to teaching young people about wolves and wolf endangerment. The group has created three different age levels of reading materials for children, and in 1991 it began an educational outreach program in thirty schools in Washington State.

At home in the zoo?

Another protected habitat option for wolves is zoos. Zoos can offer protection to endangered animals by removing them from potential dangers they may encounter in the wild. For endangered animals whose population is extremely low, protection from the wild may be their species' only chance to escape extinction. In addition to caring for wolves in captivity, many zoos, like wolf parks, participate in captive breeding programs that work to increase endangered wolves' populations.

For wolves, however, life in zoos is not without its drawbacks. Most zoos simply cannot provide the far-reaching territory that wolves require. People such as Robert Busch feel most American zoos lack both space and the mental stimulation wolves need to maintain the structure of pack hierarchy.

A pack of wolves that may require 300 acres will certainly function abnormally pacing around in a zoo's quarter-acre enclosure. And yet it is very common today for a large wolf pack to be contained within a very small compound, providing no escape or hiding place for the lowest-ranked members of the pack.[41]

Peter Steinhart agrees that wolves in zoos do not function as they do in the wild. "In the end," he says, "a wolf in a zoo is not a wolf. It is the interaction of genes and environment that makes a species, and the whole complex

El Lobo, the Mexican wolf, no longer survives in the wild. These Mexican wolves, held up by a zookeeper, were born in captivity.

interplay of thousands of such processes that makes an ecosystem. If we lock wolves up in zoos, we stop their interactions. We change their evolution."[42]

Many zoos around the country have made special efforts to redesign animal exhibits so that they are very similar to natural habitats. Limited space is almost always an issue, however, and without their normal range of territory and opportunities to hunt, both important aspects of pack life, wolves become bored in zoos. And people, Steinhart writes, become bored with them. The maximum visitor viewing time spent outside wolf exhibits is about thirty seconds, he says, because

> to see a wolf in a zoo is to see a picture of a wolf. It's not doing anything. People howl at it or shout "Lobo!," but it doesn't lift its head, doesn't even crack open an eye. The wolf has heard all this a hundred times a day for years and is bored by it. And people aren't entranced by their own reflected boresomeness.[43]

Although some biologists fear that wolf captivity alters wolves both behaviorally and, after periods of time, genetically, captive breeding programs in zoos and elsewhere are essential for saving some wolf species that have not recovered their population numbers in the wild. By providing a safe, temporary habitat for wolves, such as the pair of rare Mexican wolves in the breeding program at the Rio Grande Zoo in Albuquerque, New Mexico, zoos give species a chance to live in a secure environment.

Currently, no Mexican wolves survive in the wild, but the Rio Grande Zoo and other facilities have done much to help prevent the extinction of the species. At the Rio Grande Zoo, forty-four wolf pups had been born in captivity as of 1995. All of these wolves survived. Once the population level reaches one hundred, the zoo plans to begin releasing the wolves back into the wild.

Wolves as pets

The protected lands of national parks or wolf parks afford wolves the most freedom to roam, hunt, and live within the social structure of their packs in natural settings.

Although zoos may not be the best habitat option, endangered wolves living in a zoo are likely to be properly cared for, protected, and given a chance to increase in number. This level of care is less certain when a wolf is raised as a pet in a private home.

Some of the people who have pet wolves are drawn to them by the idea of owning an exotic, wild animal. Others believe they are aiding wolf conservation efforts by protecting their wolf from potential hazards in the wild. Many environmentalist groups, including the International Union for the Conservation of Nature and Natural Resources (IUCN), feel that wolf ownership actually threatens wolf conservation. Research shows that wolf owners often abandon wolves raised as pets. For this reason, the IUCN recommends that governments prohibit, or at least strictly regulate, interbreeding between wolves and dogs and the keeping of wolves and wolf hybrids as pets.

Robert Busch believes that the trend of wolf and wolf-hybrid ownership is a serious issue that must be addressed. "Wild animals belong in the wild, not in one's home. No

Although this little girl does not seem threatened by her pet wolf, private wolf ownership is a controversial issue among environmentalists, wolf-hybrid breeders, and wolf owners.

domestic situation can fulfill the mental and physical needs of a wild animal, no matter how much that animal is loved by its owner."[44]

Wolves kept as pets often become stressed and neurotic because of confinement in areas much smaller than their nature demands. Even raised around humans from birth, wolves cannot always be trained, especially where hunting behavior is concerned. "They simply do not understand that the neighbor's poodle is not fair game,"[45] Busch says.

Wolf owners are often surprised when wolves act more like wolves than the dogs they have been raised to be. When pet wolves reveal their wild nature, wolf owners often respond by trying to return them to the wild or offering them to zoos.

Wolf-dog hybrids

Like domestically raised wolves, wolf-dog hybrids have less of a chance of surviving in the wild than purebred, wild wolves. Hybrids released in the wild also threaten the genetic purity of wild wolves if they breed within wild packs. Zoos are not an option for hybrids, as zoo officials are often unable to introduce these pets into established zoo packs. The result, Busch says, is that "all too often, the animal ends its short life being humanely euthanized, or being placed in a third-rate zoo or game farm."[46]

According to the Humane Society of the United States, more than three hundred thousand wolf-dog hybrids are currently kept as pets in America. Wolf hybrids have become a popular trophy pet among those who want to own something exotic and wild. Like keeping wolves as pets, however, keeping wolf hybrids can be dangerous, as hybrids are still part wild wolf.

The debate over wolf-hybrid ownership is ongoing. Breeders fight for the right to produce the animals for a market of individuals that continues to demand them. Those against hybrid ownership, including most wolf conservation organizations, argue that prohibiting wolf-hybrid ownership is the most humane and logical thing to do for the sake of the animals and humans alike.

Although many wolf owners claim to be supporting wolf conservation by affording their pets protection they would not have in the wild, biologists find that private wolf ownership does nothing to rectify wolf endangerment. In fact, it often contributes to endangerment in that each time wolf owners release their wolves in the wild, the genetic purity of the established wild population is threatened. When wolf hybrids mate with wild wolves, the pups born in the wild are also part hybrid; genetic purity is thus altered.

One of the first people to breed wolf hybrids, Terry Jenkins explains that some people choose wolf hybrids because it is as close as they will ever come to owning a real wolf. Although Jenkins went into breeding with the hopes of producing animals that looked as beautiful as wolves but acted like domestic dogs, what she found was, "if it looks like a wolf, doggone it, it acts like a wolf." Jenkins eventually learned that her wolf hybrids did not make ideal pets. They needed more living space than her dogs, and unlike dogs, they needed a consistent diet of raw meat. In addition, she says, "They aren't good guard dogs because they don't bark at strangers. They shed like buffalo and almost always suffer from diarrhea."[47]

Wolf owners are often surprised that raising wolves as pets does not necessarily constrain their wild nature.

In addition to their special living quarters and dietary needs, wolf hybrids are also more aggressive than their pure wolf counterparts. Canine fatal-attack statistics compiled by the Humane Society rank wolf hybrids in sixth place, behind malamutes, huskies, shepherds, Rottweilers, and pit bulls. Pit bulls killed sixty-seven people between 1979 and 1994, while hybrids killed twelve people—all of them children—during the same period. Louis Sahagun adds that although the rate of attack seems infrequent in comparison with pit bull attacks, "as one state legislative analysis points out, since there are fewer hybrids, their percentage of fatal attacks is higher."[48]

Patti Nickerson, never a hybrid owner herself, is one mother who lost her five-year-old daughter to a wolf-hybrid attack in 1989. She is currently lobbying for a bill in her home state of Michigan that will restrict wolf-hybrid ownership.

> I am appalled that people are mixing wolves and dogs. And what for? Money and ego. It's despicable. The animal that killed my daughter was a freak. The dog side didn't fear people. The wolf side was a high-strung stalker. Put those things together and you had a schizophrenic monster.[49]

Responsible owners

Despite stories of vicious attacks, there are plenty of hybrid breeders in the United States who are continuing the practice. Pat Carney, for instance, is a past president of the National Hybrid Association that is working to keep hybrid breeding and ownership legal in the United States. She claims that problems arise not from the hybrids themselves but from the people who own them.

Carney stresses the need for large enclosures, for example, as she believes a hybrid's temperament changes only when it has been chained up. Breeder Kay Simmons agrees, stipulating that a minimum yard size of fifty by fifty feet, a six-foot fence, and a special breed of person are requirements for hybrid ownership. Simmons, who owns fifty hybrids herself, says, "Most people are not evolved enough to deserve hybrids—weirdos are drawn to them. Out of a hundred people who want one, maybe one person should have one."[50]

Wolf habitat in the future

Humankind has learned much about the effects of habitat destruction on wolves. Whether lost from natural causes, such as floods and droughts, or human causes, such as industrial pollution and development, it has witnessed the shrinking of wilderness, the loss of wolf territory, and subsequently, the endangerment of various wolf species. Conservationists and biologists have learned through habitat loss that if wolves are to be saved for future generations to enjoy, their natural habitats must also be protected. Where habitat protection is no longer possible, however, the best alternative is to provide new habitat that closely mirrors life in the wild.

5

Saving the Wolf

HAD IT NOT been for the legal protections provided by the Endangered Species Act (ESA) that took effect in 1973, the dwindling population of wolves in the United States would have easily become extinct. Today, endangered wolf populations are not only protected under the ESA, they are receiving the additional assistance of recovery-and-reintroduction programs, which work to bolster wolf population numbers and then reintroduce wolves back into protected, wild environments.

Under the Endangered Species Act, the Fish and Wildlife Service and the National Marine Fisheries Service have the power to oversee the protection and conservation of all wolves listed as endangered or threatened. As is the case with other endangered species, listed wolves may not be removed from their protected areas, and it is illegal to "harass, harm, pursue, hunt, shoot, wound, kill, trap, capture, or collect" them. In addition, "their parts, or any products made from them may not be imported, exported, possessed, or sold."[51]

While protection under the ESA has benefited some wolves in the wild, as in the cases of the red wolf and Mexican wolf populations, so few animals remain in the wild that protection alone is not enough. Without help from outside forces, these rapidly thinning populations will die from natural causes, and their species will become extinct. This fact led to the development of recovery-and-reintroduction programs aimed at restoring health to wolf populations.

Recovery and reintroduction

The process of restoring endangered and threatened animals is known as recovery and reintroduction, or simply recovery. Wolf recovery programs are run by the Fish and Wildlife Service, with help from federal and state biologists and other experts.

Recovery efforts usually involve captive breeding programs that help a species regain its population numbers. These programs are especially important for wolves whose numbers are so small that they are no longer mating in the wild or for those that are weakening the genetic purity of the species by mating with coyotes or dogs. Once the captive breeding programs have run their course and the wolves are deemed healthy enough to survive on their own, they are slowly reintroduced back into protected areas in the wild.

Today, 149 Mexican wolves survive in breeding programs. Without legal protection and recovery efforts, this wolf species would be extinct.

Gray wolf recovery success in Yellowstone and elsewhere

By far, the most publicized and most successful reintroduction story has been that of the return of the gray wolf to Yellowstone National Park. According to author Sharon Begley, the gray wolf's reintroduction marks "one of the few times that the ESA has been used to return a top-of-the-food-chain predator to lands from which it had been eliminated."[52]

The first stage of reintroduction took place in November 1994, after more than 150 public hearings, $12 million spent in scientific studies, and 160,000 public comments made on the matter. Once the debates on the issues subsided, biologists went forward with their plans of removing wolves from Canada—where wolves are plentiful—and relocating them in the United States. Biologists paid Canadian trappers to capture thirty wolves and fit them with radio collars. After these wolves were fitted, biologists transported fifteen wolves to the Yellowstone area and fifteen to Idaho. When they reached their destinations, the wolves were placed in large holding pens for ten weeks to give them a chance to acclimate to their new surroundings. Finally, in January 1995, with their radio collars still in place for tracking and monitoring purposes, they were set free in the wild. The U.S. Fish and

As part of the Yellowstone wolf reintroduction program, a U.S. Fish and Wildlife Service employee retrieves a sedated wolf from its holding pen.

Wildlife Service reports that most of these wolves adapted well to their new surroundings by engaging in normal hunting and breeding behaviors.

Making some compromises

Residents of communities located near the release areas have expressed strong concerns about the presence of these wolves. Compromises between wolf conservationists and the public, however, have helped stem these fears. The Yellowstone and Idaho wolves are listed as "experimental" populations, meaning they do not have all of the ESA protection granted to other endangered animals. For example, ranchers can kill experimental wolves that threaten livestock. In other circumstances, the killing of endangered wolves is strictly illegal.

Monetary compensation funds also give ranchers and other landowners some help when wolves stray from their new reintroduction territories. Hank Fischer, an administrator of the Defenders of Wildlife Wolf Compensation Fund, says that the goal of wolf groups like Defenders is "to have wolf supporters take responsibility for wolf indiscretions."[53] This responsibility takes the form of money paid to ranchers for wolf predation of livestock.

The U.S. Fish and Wildlife Service initially estimated that with the reintroduction of 100 wolves, 19 cows and 68 sheep would be lost each year in the Yellowstone area, and 10 cows and 57 sheep would fall in Idaho. Research, however, suggests that the loss rates for the last ten years have been much lower.

Those ranchers who do lose livestock due to wolf predation are compensated for the value of their lost animals. One rancher in Montana, for example, received $961 for his loss of six ewes and two lambs. In Idaho, another rancher received $347 for a calf. From 1987 to July 1996, twenty-eight ranchers had been compensated for wolf predation. The fund paid out $21,995 for forty-five cattle and twenty-one sheep. Fischer says his group hopes this "solid record of responsiveness brings the one thing we seek in exchange: tolerance on the part of ranchers and other

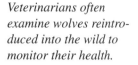

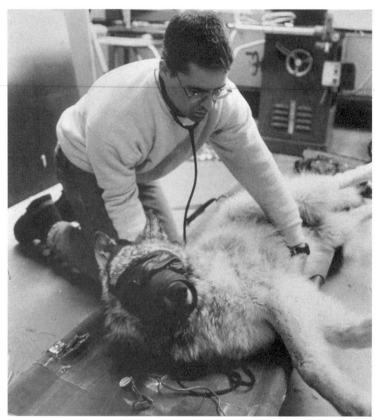

members of the public for wolves that do not bother their livestock. We remain committed to upholding our side of the bargain."[54]

Back in the wild

With its large range of territory and abundance of prey, such as elk and bison, Yellowstone has proven itself as an ideal habitat for the newly reintroduced wolves. Of the three original packs released in 1995 in Yellowstone, two have set up permanent residence in the park. The other pack has ventured outside Yellowstone boundaries but remains within the "recovery zone," the area assigned for wolf reintroduction. One of the three packs has also given birth to eight pups, which is a good sign, as it shows the wolves are breeding and are able to increase their population on their own.

Despite the success illustrated at Yellowstone, the reintroduction program has experienced some setbacks. One wolf was killed after it preyed on local sheep. Another adult wolf was found shot, and one of the eight pups born in Yellowstone was run over by a truck. In Idaho, some of the wolves have also died of various causes, but these losses are well below the 50 percent mortality rate originally predicted by some biologists. The actual losses are not significant enough to render the reintroduction program a failure, but every loss does count since the wolf population is not yet thriving; it still retains its endangered status. The recovery program itself has suffered financial setbacks as most of the congressional funding for the project has been cut. Private sources now keep the program running.

Additional wolves were released in both Idaho and Yellowstone in 1996 and 1997. In Yellowstone, more wolf reintroductions are planned for the next three to five years. Biologists expect that one hundred wolves will reside in the park by the year 2002. This is the same year that environmentalists hope to remove the gray wolf entirely from the endangered species list.

Other states have begun their own reintroduction programs. In Montana, for example, where reintroduced wolves are still classified as endangered, five wolf packs have established themselves. When the Montana population of wolves reaches ten breeding pairs and can maintain itself for three consecutive years in three recovery areas, these wolves will be taken off the endangered list and left to the management of the state of Montana.

Running with the red wolf

Like the gray wolf, the red wolf has started to make a comeback in the wild. The red wolf's return has been somewhat slower, but this was expected because only seventeen of four hundred wolves removed from the wild for captive breeding programs were genetically pure when the recovery process for red wolves began in the 1980s. The others turned out to be coyote-wolf hybrids and could not be used to increase red wolf numbers. Now, with thirty-seven breeding centers and two release sites, the red wolf population has climbed back to three hundred wolves in 1997.

While the majority of red wolves remain in captivity, a small number have been released in the wild. Four pairs of red wolves were reintroduced at the Alligator River National Wildlife Refuge in North Carolina in 1987. Like Yellowstone for the gray wolf, this refuge provides a healthy habitat for the red wolf, offering up ample deer, raccoons, and rabbits as prey. About sixty red wolves currently roam the refuge and outlying areas. In 1991 red wolves were released at a second site, the Great Smoky Mountains National Park in Tennessee. Twenty-six red wolves now live at that site.

The red wolf now seems to be adapting to reintroduction in the wild, but this adaptation has progressed more slowly than for the gray wolf. Aside from the small numbers of red wolves available at the beginning of the breeding program, biologists think their extended lengths of captivity have made adjustment to the wild difficult. At first, mortal-

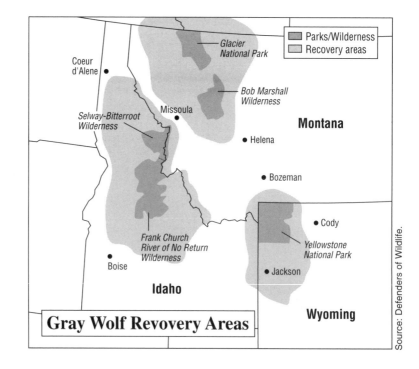

Source: Defenders of Wildlife.

Gray Wolf Revovery Areas

ity rates were high. Of forty-two wolves released, for example, twenty-two died within the first three-and-a-half years in the wild. Wolves born in the wild, however, have fared better than those bred in captivity. As of 1992, wild-born red wolves made up 63 percent of the population at the various reintroduction sites.

Despite the red wolf's seeming ability to mate and survive in the wild, management of the red wolf is likely to continue for quite a while. Biologist Michael Phillips believes that in order to maintain 220 red wolves in the wild, 320 wolves need to remain in captive breeding programs in case the wild wolves fail to reproduce. "Humans will still decide which wolves breed, which go into the wild, and which are removed from the wild. That suggests that the red wolf will never be free of human oversight and intervention."[55]

In the case of the red wolves reintroduced into North Carolina, there is some question as to whether local citizens will want to continue support for this effort. Although people working for red wolf reintroduction assured residents near the Alligator River National Refuge that the wolves would be unlikely to wander outside of the park, there have been numerous sightings of wolves in nearby local communities.

Congressman Walter Jones, who represents many of the affected communities, is working to repeal the $350,000 annual congressional allocation for the red wolf program. A member of Jones's staff states, "This has become an extremely serious problem in our district. In some areas, people see them [red wolves] quite frequently and they are understandably reluctant to allow their pets and children to go outside."[56]

The special case of El Lobo, the Mexican wolf

Another wolf population receiving necessary human intervention is the Mexican wolf, El Lobo. The Mexican wolf, which once roamed the mountain regions of Mexico and the southern borders of Arizona, New Mexico, and Texas, was declared an endangered species in 1976. By the late 1980s it was also declared extinct in the wild.

As with the gray and red wolves, various groups have taken up the cause of the Mexican wolf. In Mexico, wolf biologist Julio Carrera feels that "there is very little hope for the Mexican wolf."[57] Carrera maintains fourteen purebred Mexican wolves in captivity but feels that even if they breed there is little land in Mexico that might actually support them, as uninhabited land is scarce and native prey is also disappearing.

Since the Mexican government has not shown interest in reintroduction programs, Carrera believes the fate of El Lobo rests with the United States. Bobbie Holaday, who heads the group Preserve Arizona's Wolves, is one person willing to take on that battle. Holaday feels that the Mexican wolf plays an important part in the Arizona landscape.

> The wolf is part of our southwestern heritage. It belongs back in the wild as part of the fabric of life. We have taken away the predators, and the wilderness areas are now void of the real essence of the wilderness, the howl of the wolf. We have

saved thousands and thousands of acres of wilderness in Arizona, but we don't have its essence. There is the wild spirit, and it's in us all. All of us have this longing for complete freedom, and what better symbol or embodiment of that than the wolf?[58]

Holaday adds that Arizona has plenty of land, water, and prey available for the reintroduction of wolves, but reintroduction efforts have been blocked.

An official ESA recovery plan was approved for the Mexican wolf in the United States in 1982. It called for reintroducing into the wild one hundred Mexican wolves bred in captivity. While the breeding goal has been met, the reintroduction aspect of the plan has been delayed. This delay was partly caused by the concerns of hunters and ranchers, and partly by the difficulty of finding a reintroduction site that could support a new wolf population.

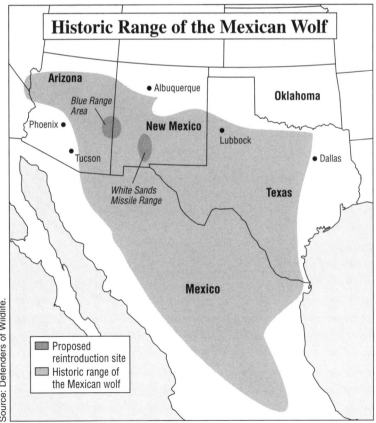

Historic Range of the Mexican Wolf

Source: Defenders of Wildlife.

Three Mexican wolf pups enjoy the shade outside their den in a wolf sanctuary.

Two areas designated as potential Mexican wolf reintroduction sites included the White Sands Missile Range in New Mexico, which is owned by the military, and the Blue Range Mountains of eastern Arizona. Biologists had expected the approval for reintroduction into one or both of these areas in 1996, but that approval has not come. Congressional cutbacks of funds for Mexican wolf reintroduction as well as a strong ranching lobby opposed to wolf reintroduction in the Southwest have been blamed for the delays.

The 149 Mexican wolves that survive today remain in captive breeding programs in zoos or wolf parks. These wolves need to be released soon. Biologists warn that for every year a wolf spends in captivity its chances of survival in the wild decrease. In 1997, reintroduction of the Mexican wolf was still an unattained goal, although biologists hope to release the wolves sometime in 1998. At present, the Mexican wolf's future does not look as hopeful as its gray wolf cousin's.

America says "yes" to saving the wolf

Wolf recovery-and-reintroduction programs have allowed wolf populations to steadily increase, and many citizens, it seems, are happy about this fact. In national and regional attitude surveys conducted since the wolf's listing as an endangered species, Americans have voiced their approval of wolves and reintroduction programs.

In one national survey in the 1990s, for example, 56 percent of Americans supported efforts aimed at saving the wolf. Likewise, Americans expressed approval of the wolf's return to Yellowstone National Park by nearly a two-to-one margin. Participants in this poll liked knowing that wolves would be present again in Yellowstone and that visitors would have the opportunity to see wolves or perhaps to hear them howl. Some respondents agree that the wolf is worth saving simply because it is endangered, and others said they "value the wolf as a symbol of nature's beauty and feel it contributes to the wildness of the outdoor experience."[59]

Some residents of communities near wolf reintroduction sites also say they appreciate the monetary benefit of the wolf's return. National parks reap the rewards of increased tourism, and towns in these areas have witnessed increases in sales of wolf-related merchandise. Wolf reintroduction in Yellowstone National Park alone is expected to generate more than $20 million annually from visitors hoping to see wolves.

The opposition cries wolf

Not everyone is pleased with the return of the wolf. One concern involves cost. The Fish and Wildlife Service spends an estimated $65,000 per animal in its reintroduction program. This is a high cost to pay when there are no guarantees that reintroduction will stabilize population numbers.

Even some environmentalists feel that the cost of saving wolves is too extreme. For example, a Sierra Club lawsuit that argued against reintroduction noted that the gray wolves have been migrating into the United States on their own from Canada for a number of years. "Some have already reached Montana," Valerie Richardson writes, "and wolf packs are expected to settle in Yellowstone in about thirty years."[60] The Sierra Club believes that wolves should not be taken from Canada to speed up population growth in the United States. That organization believes nature should be allowed to take its course and that humankind can view or study wolves elsewhere until they return to the United States.

Many ranchers also oppose wolf reintroduction programs. Beautiful or not, the wolf is still a predator, a potential threat to livestock and ranchers' livelihood. Many of these ranchers, Steinhart notes, are old enough to remember mass wolf extermination programs that were in place when they were children and still fear the wolf:

"EXCUSE ME. SEC. BABBIT...THERE'S ANOTHER GROUP OUT HERE OPPOSED TO RELEASING WOLVES BACK INTO THE WILD..."

In a national survey conducted during the 1990s, 56 percent of Americans expressed support for saving the wolf.

At a public hearing in Helena, one rancher compared releasing wolves in the park [Yellowstone] to dumping hazardous waste in a suburban neighborhood. The president of the Montana Woolgrowers Associated declared, "Anything that has blood in its veins will be a target for wolves!" A rancher from Jordan, Montana, said, "On our ranch, we lose from ten to one hundred lambs every year to coyotes. Nobody in their right mind would introduce the wolf, which is a far worse predator than a coyote. . . . We in agriculture will protect our livestock and our private property from all predators, by any means possible. No wolves, nowhere!" [61]

Anticipating the success of future reintroduction programs, environmentalists hope to remove the gray wolf from the endangered species list by the year 2002.

Ranchers fear wolf reintroduction as infringing on private property rights. They worry that wolves will wander onto their land and, because wolves are protected under the ESA, ranchers will have no rights on their own land to protect their livestock. Jason Campbell, natural resource coordinator for the Montana Stockgrowers Association, notes that ranchers in his state are fairly accepting of wolves relocating from Canada on their own. "But when a federal agency is bringing them in and basically sticking them in your backyard that gets a little bit tough for our people to understand. Private property rights are a big issue here."[62] Indeed, wolves do not know boundaries. They have no way of knowing which lands are protected and which are private. Thus when wolves stray, and the government prohibits ranchers from responding, ranchers feel their own rights are secondary to the rights given to wolves.

The future of the wolf

Some people may always oppose wolf reintroduction programs and feel, perhaps, that the habitat needs of the wolf should not receive priority over the needs of humans. But others have offered support efforts to save the wolf. Renee Askins writes that our attitude toward and treatment of wolves directly reflects our attitudes toward the natural world.

> Wolves mean something to everyone. But in the end, wolves are only wolves. The real issue is one of making room, and there is still a little room . . . room for hunters, for environmentalists, for ranchers, and for wolves.[63]

Notes

Chapter 1: Demystifying the Wolf

1. Nancy Jo Tubbs, "Cry Wolf: Tracking Down an Alleged Wolf Attack on a Human," in Rick McIntyre, ed., *War Against the Wolf: America's Campaign to Exterminate the Wolf.* Stillwater, MN: Voyageur, 1995, p. 353.

2. McIntyre, *War Against the Wolf,* p. 357.

3. Robert H. Busch, *The Wolf Almanac.* New York: Lyons & Burford, 1995, p. 45.

4. Busch, *The Wolf Almanac,* p. 44.

5. Busch, *The Wolf Almanac,* p. 52.

6. Quoted in Busch, *The Wolf Almanac,* p. 28.

7. Jim Brandenburg, *To the Top of the World: Adventures with Arctic Wolves.* New York: Walker and Company, 1993, p. 26.

8. Quoted in Busch, *The Wolf Almanac,* p. 49.

9. Busch, *The Wolf Almanac,* p. 64.

10. Brandenburg, *To the Top of the World,* p. 24.

11. Candace Savage, *The World of the Wolf.* San Francisco: Sierra Club Books, 1996, p. 54.

12. Busch, *The Wolf Almanac,* p. 65.

13. L. David Mech, "Wolf Pack Witness: Research on Arctic Wolf Behavior," *Audubon,* vol. 98, no. 6, November/December 1996, p. 82.

Chapter 2: The Great Hunter

14. Rick Bass, "Links in the Chain," *Sports Illustrated,* vol. 82, no. 25, June 26, 1995, p. 13.

15. Bass, "Links in the Chain," p. 13.

16. Quoted in Busch, *The Wolf Almanac,* p. 84.

17. L. David Mech, *The Wolf: The Ecology and Behavior of an Endangered Species.* New York: Natural History Press, 1970, p. 264.

18. Mech, *The Wolf,* p. 279.

19. Savage, *The World of the Wolf,* p. 90.

20. Savage, *The World of the Wolf,* p. 89.

21. Savage, *The World of the Wolf,* p. 89.

22. Quoted in "Top 10 Lies About the ESA," Defenders of Wildlife website, 1997, http://www.defenders.org/esatop.html.

23. Quoted in Peter Steinhart, *The Company of Wolves.* New York: Knopf, 1995, p. 233.

24. Quoted in Steinhart, *The Company of Wolves,* p. 236.

25. Quoted in William K. Stevens, "Wolves' Howl Could Return to Adirondacks," *New York Times,* November, 17, 1997.

26. Robert M. McClung, *Lost Wild America: The Story of Our Extinct and Vanishing Wildlife.* North Haven, CT: Shoe String Press, 1993, pp. 123–24.

27. Mech, *The Wolf,* p. 300.

28. Quoted in Chris Horne, "Wolf Update: Reintroduction of Wolves in Yellowstone National Park," *American Forests,* vol. 102, no. 2, Spring 1996, p. 42.

29. Renee Askins, "Releasing Wolves from Symbolism: Excerpts from Testimony Before the House Committee on Resources," *Harper's Magazine,* vol. 290, no. 1,739, April 1995, p. 17.

Chapter 3: Wolf as Prey

30. Steinhart, *The Company of Wolves,* p. 36.

31. Steinhart, *The Company of Wolves,* p. 37.

32. McClung, *Lost Wild America,* p. 126.

33. McClung, *Lost Wild America,* p. 124.

34. Savage, *The World of the Wolf,* p. 94.

35. Quoted in Busch, *The Wolf Almanac,* p. 117.

36. McClung, *Lost Wild America,* p. 125.

37. Quoted in Bill Sherwonit, "Wolf Showdown in Alaska," Defenders of Wildlife website, 1997, http://www.defenders.org/su96akw1.html.

38. Quoted in Sherwonit, "Wolf Showdown in Alaska," Defenders of Wildlife website.

Chapter 4: Habitat Destruction and the Search for New Homes

39. Bass, "Links in the Chain," p. 13.

40. "The National Park Service Program," *Park Net,* National Park Service website, 1997, http://www.nps.gov/.

41. Busch, *The Wolf Almanac,* p. 138.

42. Steinhart, *The Company of Wolves,* p. 210.

43. Steinhart, *The Company of Wolves,* p. 207.

44. Busch, *The Wolf Almanac,* p. 149.

45. Busch, *The Wolf Almanac,* p. 150.

46. Busch, *The Wolf Almanac,* p. 150.

47. Quoted in Louis Sahagun, "Modern-Day Frankenstein: Human's Romanticized Notions and Wolves' Primitive Instincts Create a Nightmarish Hybrid," *Los Angeles Times Magazine,* August 17, 1997, p. 14.

48. Sahagun, "Modern-Day Frankenstein," p. 16.

49. Quoted in Sahagun, "Modern-Day Frankenstein," p. 18.

50. Quoted in Sahagun, "Modern-Day Frankenstein," p. 18.

Chapter 5: Saving the Wolf

51. "How the ESA Works," Defenders of Wildlife website, 1997, http://www.defenders.org/esahow.html.

52. Sharon Begley, "The Return of the Native," *Newsweek,* vol. 125, no. 4, January 23, 1995, p. 53.

53. Quoted in "Wolf Compensation Trust," Defenders of Wildlife website, 1997, http://www.defenders.org/wolfcomp.html.

54. Quoted in "Wolf Compensation Trust," Defenders of Wildlife website.

55. Quoted in Steinhart, *The Company of Wolves,* p. 190.

56. Quoted in Alston Chase, "Game of Chance with the Wolf Pack," in Brenda Stalcup, ed., *Endangered Species.* San Diego: Greenhaven Press, 1996, pp. 147–48.

57. Quoted in Steinhart, *The Company of Wolves,* p. 211.

58. Quoted in Steinhart, *The Company of Wolves,* p. 195.

59. Quoted in "Wolf Prints VI," Defenders of Wildlife website, 1997, http://www.defenders.org/wp100996.html.

60. Valerie Richardson, "Decrying Wolves (Returning the Gray Wolf to the Rocky Mountain West)," *National Review,* vol. 47, no. 5, March 20, 1995, p. 28.

61. Steinhart, *The Company of Wolves,* p. 260.

62. Quoted in Mary Nemeth, "Wolves in the Wild: A Relocation Program Draws Ranchers' Wrath," *Maclean's,* vol. 109, no. 7, February 12, 1996, p. 79.

63. Askins, "Releasing Wolves from Symbolism," p. 17.

Glossary

---

biosphere: The environment in which we live.

bounty: A payment to encourage the destruction of dangerous animals.

canid: An animal related to dogs, such as wolves, jackals, and foxes.

carrion: Dead flesh.

euthanized: To be put to sleep (death).

fecundity: Fruitful in the production of offspring.

hybrid: An offspring of two animals of different species.

nomadic: Roaming from place to place.

predacide: A combination of chemicals used especially to poison predatory animals.

predation: The act of preying on animals for food.

predator: An animal that survives by preying on others.

strychnine: A poison.

ungulate: Any animal that has hooves.

Organizations to Contact

Defenders of Wildlife
1244 19th St. NW
Washington, DC 20036
(202) 682-9400

Defenders of Wildlife is concerned with the protection of all native wild animals and plants in their natural habitats. Focus is on the accelerating rate of extinction of species, loss of biological diversity, and habitat alteration and destruction.

National Wildlife Federation
1400 16th St. NW
Washington, DC 20036-2266
(202) 797-6800

The National Wildlife Federation promotes conservation and appreciation of wildlife and natural resources worldwide.

U.S. Fish and Wildlife Service
Office of Public Affairs
1849 C St. NW
Washington, DC 20240
(202) 208-5634

The U.S. Fish and Wildlife Service works to conserve and protect fish, wildlife, and their natural habitats. The service maintains information on the Endangered Species Act.

Wolf Haven International
3111 Offut Lake Rd.
Tenino, WA 98589
(360) 264-4695

Open to the public, Wolf Haven is a wolf park that provides sanctuary for unwanted, once-captive wolves. The education center at Wolf Haven conducts ecology classes and tours of the sixty-five-acre grounds, and sponsors an adopt-a-wolf program through which wolf enthusiasts can support wolves at the park.

World Wildlife Fund
1250 25th St. NW
Washington, DC 20037
(202) 293-4800

The World Wildlife Fund works to save endangered species, conduct wildlife research, and improve the natural environment.

Suggestions for Further Reading

Jim Brandenburg, *To the Top of the World: Adventures with Arctic Wolves.* New York: Walker and Company, 1993. Wildlife photographer Jim Brandenburg writes about his visits to Ellesmere Island in Canada's Northwest Territories, where he filmed a pack of Arctic wolves over several months. Includes color photos of Arctic wolves.

Robert H. Busch, *The Wolf Almanac.* New York: Lyons & Burford, 1995. Robert Busch is a longtime researcher of wolves. In this thorough look at wolves he includes elements of wolf lore, biological facts, and expert testimony about wolf behavior. Includes black-and-white and color photos.

Robert M. McClung, *Lost Wild America: The Story of Our Extinct and Vanishing Wildlife.* North Haven, CT: Shoe String Press, 1993. McClung traces the history of wildlife conservation and environmental politics in America, and describes various extinct or endangered species.

Candace Savage, *The World of the Wolf.* San Francisco: Sierra Club Books, 1996. Savage is an award-winning natural history writer. In this book she examines wolf pack structure, sex roles, communication, and hunting strategies. She also discusses current conservation efforts. Includes color photographs.

Roland Smith, *Journey of the Red Wolf.* New York: Dutton, 1996. This sixty-page book was written for young readers. It includes many color pictures of red wolves and examines red wolf biology and behavior, habitat destruction, and conservation efforts.

Works Consulted

"Alaska Wolf," Defenders of Wildlife website, 1997, http://www.defenders.org/akwfact.html.

Renee Askins, "Releasing Wolves from Symbolism: Excerpts from Testimony Before the House Committee on Resources," *Harper's Magazine,* vol. 290, no. 1,739, April 1995.

Rick Bass, "Links in the Chain," *Sports Illustrated,* vol. 82, no. 25, June 26, 1995.

Sharon Begley, "The Return of the Native," *Newsweek,* vol. 125, no. 4, January 23, 1995.

Cornelia B. Cessna, Nancy R. Jacobs, and Carol D. Foster, eds., *Endangered Species.* Wylie, TX: Information Plus, 1994.

Alston Chase, "Game of Chance with the Wolf Pack." In Brenda Stalcup, ed., *Endangered Species.* San Diego: Greenhaven Press, 1996.

"Endangered Gray Wolf," Montana Fish, Wildlife & Parks website, 1997, http://fwp.mt.gov/wildlife/wolf.htm.

"Endangered Species: Gray Wolf," *Bilologue Series.* U.S. Department of the Interior U.S. Fish and Wildlife Service, 1995.

"Endangered Species: Red Wolf," *Bilologue Series.* U.S. Department of the Interior U.S. Fish and Wildlife Service, 1995.

Dada Gottelli and Claudio Sillero-Zubiri, "Highland Gods, but for How Long? (The Greatly Endangered Ethiopian Wolf)," *Wildlife Conservation,* vol. 97, no. 4, July/August 1994.

Chris Horne, "Wolf Update: Reintroduction of Wolves in Yellowstone National Park," *American Forests,* vol. 102, no. 2, Spring 1996.

"How the ESA Works," Defenders of Wildlife website, 1997, http://www.defenders.org/esahow.html.

Rick McIntyre, ed., *War Against the Wolf: America's Campaign to Exterminate the Wolf.* Stillwater, MN: Voyageur, 1995.

L. David Mech, *The Wolf: The Ecology and Behavior of an Endangered Species.* New York: Natural History Press, 1970.

————, "Wolf Pack Witness: Research on Arctic Wolf Behavior," *Audubon,* vol. 98, no. 6, November/December 1996.

"Mexican Wolf: The War Against El Lobo," Defenders of Wildlife website, 1997, http://www.defenders.org/lobowar.html.

"The National Park Service Program," *Park Net,* National Park Service website, 1997, http://www.nps.gov/.

Mary Nemeth, "Wolves in the Wild: A Relocation Program Draws Ranchers' Wrath," *Maclean's,* vol. 109, no. 7, February 12, 1996.

Wade Norton and Sam Palahnuk, "Wolf Haven," Norton Online, 1997, http://www.teleport.com/~wnorton/wolf.shtml.

Linda M. Rancourt, "Red Wolf Redux," *National Parks,* vol. 71, no. 5–6, May/June 1997.

"Red Wolf Reintroduction: Alligator River National Wildlife Refuge," *Federal Register,* vol. 60, no. 71, April 13, 1995.

"Restoring Wolves," *Yellowstone Wolf Facts,* Defenders of Wildlife website, 1997, http://www.defenders.org/ynpfact.html.

Valerie Richardson, "Decrying Wolves (Returning the Gray Wolf to the Rocky Mountain West)," *National Review,* vol. 47, no. 5, March 20, 1995.

Louis Sahagun, "Modern-Day Frankenstein: Humans' Romanticized Notions and Wolves' Primitive Instincts Create a Nightmarish Hybrid," *Los Angeles Times Magazine,* August 17, 1997.

Bill Sherwonit, "Wolf Showdown in Alaska," Defenders of Wildlife website, 1997, http://www.defenders.org/su96akw1.html.

Claudio Sillero-Zubiri, "The Ethiopian Wolf," *The Ethiopian Wolf Homepage,* website, 1997, http://www.scs.unr.edu/nncc/wolves/e_wolf.html.

Peter Steinhart, *The Company of Wolves.* New York: Knopf, 1995.

William K. Stevens, "Wolves' Howl Could Return to Adirondacks," *New York Times,* November 17, 1997.

"Top 10 Lies About the ESA," Defenders of Wildlife website, 1997, http://www.defenders.org/esatop.html.

"Wolf Compensation Trust," Defenders of Wildlife website, 1997, http://www.defenders.org/wolfcomp.html.

"Wolf Prints VI," Defenders of Wildlife website, 1997, http://www.defenders.org/wp100996.html.

"Wolves and Sport Hunting," Defenders of Wildlife website, 1997, http://www.defenders.org/wolfhunt.html.

Index

Picture Credits

About the Author

Hayley R. Mitchell holds a master of fine arts degree in poetry from the University of Washington and a master's degree in literature from California State University, Long Beach. Her award-winning poetry has been published in numerous literary journals throughout the United States, and she edits and publishes the small press poetry magazine *Sheila-Na-Gig.* She currently teaches composition and creative writing at various universities and community colleges in southern California and is also the author of *Teen Alcoholism,* a title in Lucent's Teen Issues series.